Volleyball Coaching Wizards - Wizard Women

Insights and experience from some of the world's great coaches

Lauren Bertolacci & John Forman

Anduril Ventures

What readers are saying

"As a female, high school volleyball coach, there are zero relatable books for our niche. Trust me, I've looked. There are numerous books for coaches of other sports, basketball, football, less books for volleyball coaching in general, but there's a huge shortage of reading material for women volleyball coaches specifically. Wizard Women fills that void. Sometimes as a coach and a leader all you need to feel better about a situation or a decision is for someone to say, yeah, I went through that too and made it out the other side. This book gives you six examples of women coaches that with their combined experience have been through it all. I found many examples, of ok, she's gone through that as well, or even ok, that's a great take on how to deal with a situation like that. Not just as a female coach, any coach could benefit from the shared wisdom in these pages." – Kassi Mortensen

"Volleyball Coaching Wizards - Wizard Women is a book every female volleyball coach should have in their volleyball library, not only to read for themselves but to share with young female athletes interested in coaching. More female coaches need to hear about these very successful coaches from so many different levels. Each of these coaches share their passion, their process in continuing to grow in their field, their love of the game, their love for their athletes and being great mentors to other women in coaching." – Brenda Williams, retired college coach

"This is a great book for coaches with all levels of experience and levels of play. The women interviewed in the book talk about how they prepare and the challenges they have faced getting their programs started. They are all very successful and built programs from the ground up while learning to successfully balance their family life. I especially enjoyed the advice they give to beginning coaches. It is amazing to me that no matter what level we coach we have some of the same challenges and obstacles but we all love our profession. This was a great learning experience for me!!" – Jamie McDougald, high school coach

"Volleyball Coaching Wizards - Wizard Women by Lauren Bertolacci and John Forman is a much needed book to help inspire more women to enter the coaching profession. As Lauren says in the book, 'I truly believe we can't be what we can't see' when referring to women in coaching. This book can serve to help rectify that problem as it showcases outstanding female coaches from around the world and a variety of levels, their individual journeys through volleyball and coaching, their evolution as coaches, and great advice for future coaches. If you are a current coach or thinking about coaching, this book will help you gain a better understanding of the profession and valuable advice moving forward." - Mark Oglesby, Georgia Volleyball Coaches Association AAA Coach of the Year 2021, 2022

Contents

What is Volleyball Coaching Wizards?   IX

Introduction to Wizard Women   XIII

The Interviews - A Quick Guide   XVII

Special Reader Bonus   XIX

1. Shannon Winzer   1

2. Erin Appleman   43

3. Audrey Cooper   73

4. Ann Schilling   107

5. Saskia Van Hintum   131

6. Denise Corlett   163

7. Bonus: Jenny McDowell   191

Please post a review   225

More Wizard Women   227

Help the Wizard Women project   229

About the Authors   231

What is Volleyball Coaching Wizards?

If you aren't already familiar with **Volleyball Coaching Wizards**, you might be wondering what exactly it's all about. Let us give you a sense of the idea and the intention.

The inspiration

Back in the late 1980s a man by the name of Jack Schwager authored a book titled *Market Wizards*. In it he shared material from a series of interviews he did with great financial market traders and investors. These individuals traded in several different markets, they had a variety of methods, and their backgrounds were diverse.

Thousands upon thousands of traders and investors consumed the original *Market Wizards* book and the follow-up editions Schwager developed over the years. They became an often re-read source of inspiration and information for a whole generation (or more) of traders. Readers could identify with the people profiled in the books and see a path to success for themselves in those pages.

The Market Wizards books also share some of the history of the markets through the eyes of those who participated in them. In that way they helped develop a trading literature above and beyond technical and tactical manuals, which are easily found.

The **Volleyball Coaching Wizards** project was conceived to fill a similar role for volleyball and volleyball coaching.

We want to give volleyball coaches the same kind of inspiration and information. We want to show how great coaches come from a variety of backgrounds. We want to show that there are great coaches operating in a wide variety of coaching arenas. We want to show that while there may be some similarities among great coaches, there is still an array of philosophies and methodologies underlying their success.

Great coaches can be found at all levels

One of the things we feel very strongly about is that coaching level does not equal coaching mastery. There is a very strong tendency to look at coaches of top national teams, outstanding professional clubs, or powerhouse college programs and say they are the best of the best. Similarly, there is a tendency to think that coaching a U18s team is higher status than coaching a U12s team because you're working with "better" players.

In other words, there's an attitude that better coaches work with better players. That leads people to think, "He/she coaches the best team, so they must be the best coach," and anyone else is less worthy of respect.

From a career perspective it leads people to think that coaching better players equates to being a better coach, which creates a ladder-climbing mentality. That isn't inherently a bad thing, of course. Moving up the ladder to bigger clubs or to universities in stronger conferences tends to mean better pay, among other things. The problem is when coaches think that because they coach at a higher level than someone else it means they are a better coach.

Coaches should be measured first and foremost by the impact they have on their players and their program or club. They should also be judged on their influence on other coaches, though admittedly those in higher profile positions will tend to have more opportunity to impact others.

A major part of being a true master coach is understanding where you can best have that influence. For some, it's at the top level of the sport. For others, though, it is at a development level.

Wizard Ruth Nelson, whose interview is featured in the first Wizards book, is a perfect example of this. She mostly coaches very young players these days. If you ever get to talk with her, though, you'll quickly realize she knows more about the sport and coaching than most. That's why she's got a steady stream of coaches seeking her mentorship. Try to tell them that since Ruth is working with a bunch of 5 year-olds she can't be considered a great coach. They'll laugh you out of the gym!

It's also a simple numbers game. There are far more coaches working with youth athletes and in low level college and club programs than there are coaches working at the elite level. There are far fewer full-time paid volleyball coaches than there are part-timers and volunteers. And when you look at places where volleyball is not as big a sport as it is elsewhere, coaches just lack the opportunity to coach elite level players - or to get paid, in many cases. They simply coach the players in front of them because they have a passion for it.

We have examples of just that among the interviews in our first book. Jefferson Williams has done most of his coaching in England where volleyball is a minor sport. Tom Turco coaches in one of the weaker volleyball regions in the U.S. From that perspective it would be easy to overlook them both. If you judge a coach on championships, however, few can come close to matching them. Equally, both have been highly influential on coaches around them.

Throw fellow Wizard Garth Pischke in there as well. He's won more men's college volleyball matches as a coach than even the legendary Al Scates. That's in Canada, though, so hardly anyone has ever heard of him. Ditto for Teri Clemens (also featured in the first book). Because she coached in Division III of the NCAA, not Division I, she doesn't have nearly the profile she could, despite having an incredible record of success.

Then there is Gerry Ford, a Wizard from Northern Ireland. It's unlikely anyone is going to think of that country when discussing volleyball. Gerry's story, though, is an example of how coaches can change lives - even potentially save them.

The point is, just because someone works at a lower level or more obscure part of the sport - either by choice or because of circumstances - it doesn't mean they should be considered a lesser coach. They should be judged on their impact and influence.

Contributing to the volleyball literature

The first thing to notice about the volleyball literature is how little of it there is. In football, or basketball, or cricket, or any number of other sports, the stories of the giants of the sport have been documented over and over again. For the most part, the lessons that can be drawn out of those sports, have been drawn out.

In volleyball - except in some small pockets - those stories have not been told. Those lessons have not been passed on. Coaches in different countries largely work on their own, seeking their inspiration from those in their small circle, or from other sports.

Our goal with the **Volleyball Coaching Wizards** project (and this series of books) is to expand those small circles into one large circle. By doing so, we can help improve the level of coaches everywhere, and grow the sport.

Introduction to Wizard Women

The whole concept of Wizard Women is interviews of successful women in coaching, by a woman, for women in coaching. As such, Lauren did all of these interviews one-on-one with each individual (aside from the bonus interview, which was done earlier). She had as an initial framework of the same basic set of topics we used in the original Wizards interviews, but with a few additions especially oriented toward female coaches. To provide some context, Lauren answered a few questions about herself and how she approached the interviews.

What was your background coming in?

I was a professional and national team player (Australia) for 10 years. As I finished my playing career I was asked to coach a men's team in Switzerland. Having never coached before, I was pretty hesitant, but it turns out it was the best choice I've made. As a coach I am more curious, relaxed, hard-working and analytical. I am a learner, constantly growing, and I can't see that ever stopping. After coaching the men in the Swiss top league for 5 years, I moved to the women's side to coach for Viteos NUC, where I still coach today. I'd had national team experience volunteering for the Australian Men and as Assistant for the Australian women leading into the interviews, and have since also been an assistant for the Canadian women. Now I lead the Swiss Women's National Team.

What attracted you to the Wizard Women project?

I truly believe we can't be what we can't see. There are far fewer women in coaching, especially at the top, which is the group that is most highly publicized. In Europe, where I am based, I can name all of them on less than one hand. If we want to engage the other half of the population, and therefore ensure we have access to even more quality coaches that we are currently missing, then we need to profile the women that are already doing the work. The more women we can see coaching, the more young women will aspire to coach, and slowly the culture changes. Then we get more and more highly skilled female coaches over time. "We just want the best candidate" is the classic argument against gender equality or quotas in any sector, and it is exactly what I try to constantly prove that we are simply not achieving. Surely, by having more women engaged in coaching we will have an even richer choice of quality coaches! This project is just one of the steps towards profiling and engaging more women in coaching, and I am proud to be involved.

What do you hope readers take away from these six interviews?

Reading is just another way we can learn and engage our brains. These interviews provide extremely different perspectives, they show different styles and philosophies of coaching, and give a unique female perspective on the coaching job. I am sure they will inspire readers to think differently, assess their own coaching philosophies and above all make us proud that there are some really great women at all levels of the game.

What did you get out of these interviews?

I had a lot of fun doing these interviews. Preparing and researching for them was a long process, but I already learned a lot before we even got to the interview. Each woman that I talked to came from a different background, with a different family life, and has faced different adversities. What stood out the most for me was that where each coach is now is a totally different place to where they were when they started. Learning is important, embracing growth is key, and being able to challenge your own ideas and reflect is the only way forward. These women all used their past experiences to become better coaches and grow their players, and I thought that was very inspiring.

A note on the interviews

What you will see in the chapters to follow are transcripts of the conversations Lauren had with each coach. If you've ever seen a transcript of a conversation or interview, you know it's not always an easy read. We all have our conversational quirks in terms of how we transition between thoughts. We're all guilty of running on our sentences, or starting on one thought, then shifting to another midway through. That's usually easy to follow in conversation, but can make for difficult reading.

For the sake of readability each interview has been edited as appropriate. That means while what you see will mostly be word-for-word what the Wizard coach said, but in places things are smoothed out in terms of grammar, punctuation, etc. The intention was always to maintain the interviewee's voice and tone, and definitely not to alter the content of what they said. So you will sometimes see where they started to say something, then changed gears a bit.

Note that Lauren conducted these interviews in mid-2020 (you can blame John for not getting them published sooner). This is after most seasons had been shut down due to covid, but before that also impacted the 2020-21 seasons around the world. As a result, you won't find much discussion of the subject.

The Interviews - A Quick Guide

As you'll see, each interview has a set of common questions and talking points to allow for a degree of consistency throughout, and to cover what we think are important coaching topics across all levels. That said, each coach has their own experiences and areas of focus that influences the discussion, so no two interviews are anything like the same.

We know that readers don't tend to go through books like this straight through from front to back. The tendency instead is to pick out the most interesting first, then go back to the others afterwards. While we strongly suggest at least reading the Shannon Winzer interview first, as it was the first Lauren did and lays a kind of foundation for the others, that's by no means a requirement.

With that in mind, here's a quick guide to the interviews. It isn't comprehensive in terms of all the subjects covered, but gives a flavor of some of the high points.

Shannon Winzer - A Canadian who started at the adult club level and progressed to national team coaching. In her interview she talks about the evolution of coaching practices, how her philosophy developed from being a player to a coach, and the importance of mentors in coaching and development.

Erin Appleman – A US college coach. Her interview focuses a lot on changing/developing a culture, recruiting philosophy, and ideas to making coaching more accessible as a career option for young mothers.

Audrey Cooper – A Scot who led Team GB in the 2012 Olympics and has coached both professional and non-professional adult club teams. She shares her experience transitioning from player to coach, being guided by your philosophy, and developing a team identity.

Ann Schilling – A US high school and juniors coach. Her interview focuses a lot on growing and evolving as a coach, and shares her experience battling cancer.

Saskia Van Hintum – A Dutch coach who's worked across the levels from juniors to pro and national team indoors, and at the national team level on the beach. She shares a comparison of beach and indoor coaching, the influence of being a high level player on her coaching, and the importance of coaching your way.

Denise Corlett – A US college assistant coach. Her interview talks a lot about being a career long-assistant coach, working with different head coaches, and the importance of putting the athletes first.

Jenny McDowell (Bonus) – A US college coach who at the time of publication recently stepped down after nearly 30 years. She was interviewed in the initial group of Wizards in a discussion that covers a lot of ground.

Special Reader Bonus

As a thanks for reading and supporting the Volleyball Coaching Wizards project – particularly Wizard Women – we'd like to offer you a special thank you gift. Just use the link or QR code below to claim it.

https://volleyballcoachingwizards.com/womenbonus/

Chapter One

Shannon Winzer

At the time of this interview, Canadian Shannon Winzer was the assistant coach with the Canada women's national team and head coach of the B-team and the newly formed national excellence program. Since then she's been elevated to the national team head coach. She joined Team Canada after three years as the head coach of the Australian national team in the Center of Excellence at the Australian Institute of Sport. Prior to that, she won four national league titles in Australia as a coach. In this interview Shannon shares the evolution of her coaching practices, how her philosophy developed from being a player to a coach at a high performance level, mistakes she's made and lessons she's learned the importance of mentors in coaching and development. She also discusses barriers to women's coaching – both perceived and actual - misconceptions about female coaches, and balancing a high-performance coaching job with them.

***

Can you first tell us a little bit about your history and experience in volleyball?

Well, I'm originally from Canada. We play volleyball from the age of 10 here. I went to the University of British Columbia, where I played for a few years. When I graduated, my travels took me to Europe, but I played in

England. I was probably just a mediocre player, I wasn't some high-level player. I played in the Premier League in England, and I met my husband, who happens to be Australian. I followed him back to Australia, where I played in the National League for, gosh, a long time. I kept in that team, and when I was... I played with you [Lauren] for a very long time. Then, when I finished playing there, I went from captain of the team to coaching the team, and that's where we went on to win four national championships.

The club is still really successful and I believe they're on number seven now, something like that. From there, I got picked up to Assistant Coach with Mark Barnard and the Women's National Team for Australia. Did a year and a bit with him, and then when he stepped down I took over as Head Coach with the National Team. I coached three international seasons with the Women's Volleyroos. During that time in 2017 Australia started the Center of Excellence, which is a full-time program for the top athletes coming through high school who are looking to go to the NCAA or go pro. I started that full-time program with Australia, and I ran that for two years while I was still with the national team. Then, I got offered a job with Team Canada, so I jumped back home last year... just over a year ago today.

I'm coaching with Tom Black and Team Canada. I'm Assistant Coach with the National Team, Head Coach of what's called Next Gen, which is the B team. Those are the athletes who we expect to be 4-8 years out of podium. And we're also starting a full-time program for the National Excellence program – 2028 Olympians. We start that program in September, and so I've just finished a huge recruiting and talent identification for that. That's where I am now, in Canada with the Senior National Team and trying to qualify for 2024.

Can you tell us a little bit about the Australian league, how it works? I can't imagine that too many people would have a great understanding of that.

Sure. I don't know where it's at now. It's changed so much over the years. I think back when we played – and still to this day – there was one team per state. You represent your state. It's the senior level. It used to be part of the pathway to the Senior National Team, so you had to play for your state to basically be an option for the Senior National Team as it developed. It still was the highest level in Australia and we still identified players through that. However, we used the pro leagues in Europe and Asia as a pathway to the Senior National Team rather than just the National League. But, you go around the country, you play each state, it's a league that finishes in the National Championship.

It runs over… Back in the day was over four or five months. Now, it's quite small. It's not as long.

Professional, or?

No, not professional. I mean, I was paid as a coach, but maybe enough to cover my gas. And players paid. We played for a club that was really heavily supported by the university. It was Melbourne University who supported the program, so our player's fees weren't very big. However, some of the other states had huge fees. So no, not professional, but it was the highest level in Australia, and it's all we have. At the very minimum, we expected players to play that, but obviously we wanted players to leave Australia to go and play.

The Next Gen program… How long do you have girls for? Is it a full-time program for you? Or are they just in a program? What does it mean exactly?

Well, the Next Gen program that I coach is our Senior B team, so they're still part of the Senior National Team. We have essentially 32 athletes across the whole national team. So, our athletes are paid monthly, just like probably many national teams. The A team is probably about 16, maybe 18 athletes. And then, your B team, which is your Next Gen team, is that 14 to 16. The break's not that clear because we all train in the gym at roughly the same time and the coaches go across both teams. Well, I go across both teams. It's a summer program.

I like to think of our national team program as a year long program, but we're only with them face-to-face for about four months of the year. The rest of the time we're monitoring and engaging. We're doing it remotely, but it's the same as a Senior National Team program. They're the team that we took to Pan-Am Games last year. This year we had quite a few competitions lined up for them, so there's still a competition aspect. They're just usually athletes who are, like I said, 4-8 years out of podium. We're working with some who were in their first couple of years of pro, or maybe in their final two years of university. It's a huge age range. It's like 18 to 26. It's a huge age range.

Okay. Can you talk about some of your coaching influences, maybe from way back when you were a player to now?

Sure. To be honest, I think when I first started coaching I didn't give it enough thought. I think I was really influenced by my own experiences as a player. I'm not saying that's wrong, but looking back it's probably not the best approach because it really only gives you one side of the coin, and no one really shares your experiences or your perspective. I was coaching the way I wanted to be coached as a player and, well, not everybody was me. As I continued through my coaching, I really realized in the last five or six years the importance of mentors. When I was in Australia, I worked really closely with Russ Borgeaud, former Men's National Team Coach in Australia, and Dan Ilot, who was an Assistant Coach with the Australian National Team. They were fantastic mentors for me.

I also worked really, really closely with Sue Jenkins at the Australian Institute of Sport. She, to this day, is still one of my key mentors. She works with the AIS on all sport with coach development and leadership. She really works in this space with coaches across sports, and so she was invaluable for me. I see her as a mentor.

And now in Canada, I've been really lucky to be connected with a woman named Alison McNeil. She's actually quite a big name. Probably not a big name in the volleyball world, but she's the former Canadian Basketball Team head coach. She got them to the Olympics, and she was a head coach to the national team here for a long time. She's currently having a lot of influence on me and being a big support.

And there's my peers. I mean, you probably hate to hear it, but I've known you for a long time. You're someone that I ring up and ask questions and we talk about issues and we... "How would you do...? What would you do here? What are you doing there?" And that's a big one for me, so you do still have a big influence on me, even from afar.

You kind of hinted at it then, but when you said you began coaching you were more thinking as a player kind of thing. How has your coaching philosophy changed over time?

I think my coaching philosophy has always, always involved the aspect of hard work and accountability. I'm probably honest and blunt to a fault, and that's probably where some of my blind spots are. But those qualities of working hard, being accountable, having that willingness to compete, that was me as a player. I still actually really value those things as a coach. Do the things you say you're going to do, be honest even when it's hard and it's difficult, and have really clear expectations for players. But, I'd say one of the things...

I was thinking of this the other day because I spoke to a university group. One of my goals as a coach is really to create an environment where athletes can be totally fearless. I think early on in my coaching career, I hate to admit it, but I think I coached a little bit by fear. I used that fear to my advantage. And I mean, it worked. I just don't think it was going to work... it wasn't sustainable. I don't think I was going to get that from professional athletes if I continued to coach like that. I think working with an amateur athlete you can get away with coaching by fear a little bit, or using fear as a motivator. I can't believe I'm admitting that, but when you start to work with a higher level athlete I just don't think it works. I really don't think it works. So, creating an environment where an athlete can be fearless, where they feel like they can push the limits, take risks, and grow and learn and not be afraid of consequences – I think that's when you create this environment where they go way beyond what they thought was capable.

That's really my goal. I don't think I have it down pat, but that's really what I would want to achieve as a coach. But then, that kind of unpacks a lot more like when an athlete can be fearless or when you have an environment that you want them to be fearless in.

You also need to have trust. They need to have trust. You need to have effective communication. Obviously, accountability. If you say you want to push the limits, but then you punish errors, my actions aren't in line with my goal. If an athlete says they want the team to succeed at the highest level, but then they're not putting in at practice, they're not working hard, they're dogging it in the gym, well, then their actions aren't in line with the goal. So, this all affects our ability to trust.

I also think if we... To have trust, an athlete and your staff also need to know that you care. I don't actually hear coaches talk about caring enough. I think an athlete needs to feel that they are safe with you, and that you'll look after them, and that you want what they want, and that you care about them as a person. If you can get there with an athlete, I think the world's your oyster. So, I think that's a huge part of the trust component.

And then, obviously to be fearless, I think an athlete needs to develop... And this is probably new for me in the last couple of years, and probably new for me as a person as well, is you need to develop a really healthy relationship with failure. I think I was really scared of failure. When we coached together in Australia, I was really afraid of failing. We've had a few conversations, I remember you questioning me on it. Now, I think I'm a lot better with it, but an athlete needs to have this healthy relationship with failure and understand that, "What do my errors look like if I'm really trying to change? What will those errors look like?" And so those errors are really just a step closer to succeeding. And then, of course as a coach, my actions have to support that process. That's a lot about my philosophies, but...

It probably merges into the next thing. How do you develop concepts and culture and team-building and stuff like that?

I think being consistent is really important. You can't just pick and choose when you're going to... and that's accountability, as well. Accountability, consistency.

The big thing for right now that I think we're talking a lot with at least my Next Gen staff is that it's really important for athletes to understand the why, and for you to agree on the why. For Next Gen, it's really clear. We kind of didn't qualify for the 2020 Olympics – well now 2021 Olympics – and my job is really clearly aligned with helping us qualify for 2024. We talk about the context of Paris, 2024. How does our culture relate back to that? What actions do we want to see? I think that's really important. So, when maybe they're not pushing themselves as much... Or even just check-in. We have wellness check-ins. If you're not doing your wellness check-in so we can better manage and monitor you and plan for you and be a resource for you going forward, if you're not even doing the basics, are you really serious about 2024?

I think it's important as a group to understand the why. Why are these actions important to help us achieve the goals? Why does this little action impact the rest of the group, and how will it then eventually impact our final goal? It's important to really unpack that with the group, but then also to always come back to it. It's not something we're going to talk about in 2023 when we're qualifying. We're going to talk about it every single day at training, every day at training. We're going to talk about every drill, anytime. We want to keep it relevant, we want to keep that why relevant.

Are there other things that you guys do to get that message rammed in?

Yeah, well, I mean, I think it has to be a constant, but I also think it needs to be broken down, and how you unpack it needs to be with players. It's not me coming and going, "This is what we need to do. This, this, and this." But it's, "These are the key components: accountability, hard work, being a good learner. Okay. What does that look like?" And then they understand, and they can find the relationship between their actions and the actual part of culture. But yeah, I think it's every day.

One of the big things that we've changed – I'm attempting to change in Canada – is it's always been a goal of athletes to make the National Team, which is awesome. But how about our goal is to become an Olympian? I think that they're two very different things.

I think that you can continue what you're doing - become a professional athlete, go through NCAA or youth sport, become a professional athlete, play for your national team, and have a great professional career. You can have a great professional career without being an Olympian, but if you want to be an Olympian, what does that mean? And so, we start changing it. I talk to these athletes who are 16 years old and we're looking at them. We're trying to identify athletes for 2028. I mean, don't get me down the path of talent identification because that's just messy, but we're trying to identify athletes for 2028. And now, we're looking for 2028 Olympians. We're not looking for National Team players or professional players. Yes, that is a part of the process, but we are looking for Olympians. Just changing the mindset around that and the language, I think that's a start for us.

How do you try to worm out those kinds of players that you think have that mindset? Are there some markers that give you that indication that this girl's got what it takes to get there?

We're all lying if we say that we can be certain. There's no certainty in talent identification. There's a whole piece that our Sports Science Director is working on around gold medal profiling, which looks after your technical side of things like the physicality, but then it's also... He's doing a piece on how relevant that is to actually being successful. There's a whole piece of work there. We know that we want athletes who can play big above the net, so we're looking for the physical side of it, but the mental side and that characteristic, we're not going to know in the four hours I see them. We are going to figure it out, though, over the next four months, once we select them and we work with them day in and day out.

What I actually tell athletes is, "You can fool me in four hours, but you can't fool us for four months. At the end of those four months, we're going to have to make a decision. Are you in line with where we want to go or not?" I think that's it. I mean if it were up to me, trials for the National Team would probably last a lot longer than they are. It's just not possible in the environment we work in.

We have a large pool of athletes coming through Canada. I think there are some exceptional athletes coming through Canada, but finding those athletes who are exceptional, but also willing to compete, probably the pool's not as big. I think that willingness to compete is still a unique thing here. With our Senior National Team, obviously that's different. That's a team that, obviously they want to compete and they're there. But, when you're looking for that next group of athletes coming through, I think it's harder to find. It's also, though, part of creating an environment where they can be fearless – they're not going to be judged. There's some gender things there as well, when it comes to willingness to compete. I'm not an expert on it, but I do think that there... It's not found as commonly in women as in men. That's a personal opinion, though.

We can unpack that later. Just to jump back to the second part of coaching philosophy – like methodology – would a typical training session from when you first started coaching in the Australian league look different to what is happening now in the National Team with you?

Yeah, for sure. For sure. I mean, obviously when I first started coaching, I was doing drills that I was taught, or that I did as a player. But, if I look back on it, I think I was choosing drills that they were working hard, but wasn't transferring – like wasn't really that transferable. No one would ever complain that our trainings were soft. They were hard, for sure.

I look back and I look at drills... I think I was doing them because they also looked pretty. Were we actually transferring skills? Sometimes we just got to... I've always been fairly game-like. I've never really removed an athlete from the context of the court or the net, or anything like that. But, I think sometimes we were tossing the ball from the same side of the net, quite often. I'm like, "Well, geez! That's not very specific, is it?" I think that I've developed a lot in how I run my trainings or the drills themselves. But yeah, I look back and laugh at some of the things I did.

There's obviously a lot of talk, over a long time over motor learning principles, and I think back to when my dad used to coach me. He used to coach softball and he had no idea what motor learning principles were, but he did things because they worked. And the things that worked were things that were game-like. So, I've always had that aspect about me as a coach. But I definitely think there were drills that came in that I'm like, "What was I thinking? What were we getting out of that? Man, that drill looked good, but did it actually affect how they played in a game situation?" Probably not.

I've coached with you, so I know a lot about you and your philosophy, I'd like you to talk a little bit about the importance of coach-player relationships, and also maybe how that's changed across your career – how you've managed it and that kind of stuff.

The one thing that I don't think has changed for me is how I've held relationships really, really high. From the start of coaching to now, it's been so important to me. I think that I am a relationship-based coach. I think that my relationship with players and my staff are probably my biggest priority. I actually don't think that's changed for me, It gives us some insight into how to motivate players. It gives us some insight on how to best communicate with them. I think you can understand the context of an athlete a little bit better, and I think you need to get to know your players to work better with them. It's that aspect of caring, too. If I'm able to show I care, and I'm able to show I'm human and I'm vulnerable in front of them, they'll be more connected to me. And then, they start to trust me.

Man, once you have that strong relationship, it's like any relationship. You can start to do great things. I've really, really valued those relationships in every aspect of my coaching. When I went to a full-time program in Australia, initially I was getting athletes who I'd never worked with before, so how did I initiate those relationships was really difficult. Previously, when I went from player to coach I was coaching people I had played with or against, or I already had some level of relationship from the community or something. So that was really easy. But, then I was put up in the Australian Institute of Sport and working with athletes I had seen at a trial. How did I start to build that relationship? I started off quite formal.

I think this is something that you talked to me a lot about at the time with what you're doing with your club. I started off with these weekly meetings, and they were quite formal. It was a 10 minute catch up. We set some ground rules because in the past I was known to be a little bit reactive, so I promised to basically not talk for 10 minutes and you could take it wherever you wanted. At the very start, those meetings were superficial and we talked about the classes they were taking – really nothing to do with volleyball. I always finished the meeting with, "Hey, what can I do better for you?" I realized as a coach – probably about, I don't know, five or six years ago – the importance of getting feedback as a coach, I think I avoided it or was afraid of it for a long time.

And then, once I realized that this feedback was going to make me a better coach, and I was going to be able to develop a certain level of self-awareness and be able to self reflect, I was seeking it from everyone. That included the players. It was such a weird question for them. They would be like, "What? What do you mean? You're supposed to tell me what you're going to do. What do you mean you want to know what I want?" But then these official meetings we had every week, all of a sudden we started to get to know each other. Maybe it took six months, but all of a sudden now these are becoming really key meetings about where they're at. And I can now start having these really difficult conversations with them. Like, "I don't think you're in a hundred percent here. I don't think you're giving everything you have." And we could start to have these really big conversations because we had developed those relationships. So that was a real positive.

However, the flip side of that is because I had created this space where we were going to meet every single week. I sort of lost sight of the importance of the organic things. I obviously would be at training normally, 20 minutes before training, writing on the whiteboard and there'd be this, "Hey, well, how was class today? What are you doing?" Just having this organic kind of natural conversation. I was finding myself then being in my office that sits above the courts, doing my work right up until, because I did my whiteboard sooner, right up until everyone was ready to go. Then I'd come down and just start coaching. I realized I had neglected that organic side of building relationships I had so valued. So it was this "Aha!" moment. I used to love that. That was how I built relationships as well as these formal meetings. So I went back to making sure that I was there 20 minutes, half an hour before I started training just to shoot the shit.

Just being available, yeah.

Being available and those are the times when we have conversations outside of volleyball and maybe that's the time when they feel most comfortable addressing something with me. Not in a formal setting, but informally.

What about if you have sort of different personalities in the team, or conflict that arises between the team, or you and the team? Have you got any examples or some ways that you may have managed that in the past?

I think this is forever something that's difficult to manage. I think it's easier to manage once you have a successful culture that's built on trust because then you're judging people on their intentions more than their actions. And if you trust that people really are working towards the same goals, and they value the same things, you don't judge their actions as harshly. But yeah, I think that this is still forever going to be a struggle.

Whenever you're working with people and... I can have instances where a player needed maybe exceptional consideration or additional resources due to something that they were dealing with personally. I felt like to get the best out of that player I needed to assist and support. Then I also then had to risk how that was seen by the rest of the team. But I felt like I was doing the right thing for the team.

So how'd I manage that in hindsight? I think I still did an okay job of it. I can't really change people's perception. I can't really change what they think of it. But I still think I did a good job of unpacking it, communicating to the team best as I could over what we were dealing with and what we were putting in place to best support the player to ensure they could be their best – as a human first, and then as a volleyball player second – and how the team would benefit from it without going into the details of it. But at the end of the day, I'm still going to be judged, and I think I had to accept that.

Did you do that individually with players, or did you talk to the whole team? Because this is a situation that can arise where something special happens with a certain player. There's always that question on did you address the team or did you speak to individuals – get them on board that way? Or how did you manage that?

For majority part, I worked with a group – a leadership group. I feel like it's best working with a group of individuals who I think have the better relationships. All the athletes will then have a relationship with them. If it's a general message, or less than a sensitive message, or something I feel like I can share with the greater group directly from me, then it goes to the greater team. But for this situation, I thought it needed to be handled kind of quietly. And so I spoke to the leadership group and I just explained that if they felt like this is something they need to address. If they're hearing something in the change rooms, they know the truth. They can address it themselves. If they felt more information needed to be given, they could come back to me and let me know. But in this situation, I worked with the leadership group.

Let's jump straight into that then. What's your philosophy of selecting a leadership group? What are their responsibilities? How big would it be in relation to how big your squad is?

This is forever evolving. The way I look at leadership groups are, there's key components I want the leadership group to handle. Maybe there's an administrative aspect. There's a culture aspect. There's the team cheerleader aspects. What do I want the leadership group to achieve? And then sometimes you can find all those qualities in two humans. Maybe you can find them in three humans, but maybe you need four. I would say for a group of 12 to 14 athletes, four is even on the big side.

For a national team, I'd say, we usually worked with about four, but it was just to ensure all those aspects could be covered. Because we'd have a captain on court who was a great on-court captain. But maybe she was a bit quiet off court and didn't really do the administrative parts well, like get the team on the same board or get all the information out to the team. Or maybe she wasn't as well connected to all the athletes on the team. So it was about filling all the roles of leadership group amongst different people. And the number of people really depended on the qualities of the people I had in front of me.

Could you give me a range? What are some examples of years of how many people you had and what their exact roles were?

When I first started coaching, I had one captain. I gave way too much power to one person. I think I made that decision way too soon and it went a bit south and I had no way out then, because I had one person – probably the wrong person – have all the power. And I'm not saying just because you're captain, you have a lot of power. But in this situation, that's the way it was. So I brought in an assistant captain the next year. I had two athletes, and I thought for that group of 12 to 14 athletes, that was okay for the level I was coaching. I was coaching in the National League in Australia. I thought that actually worked okay.

But what I found then was that there were still a couple of players on the team who didn't feel connected to those two people, right? So, amongst them, they're both amazing humans. They both ticked a lot of the boxes, but there was a couple of things that were still missing. So then in the national team, we went from two to four, pretty much. And I've been with four ever since. The national team's probably a larger group though. There's probably 16 to 18 in Australia and in Canada, our B team, our Next Gen's about 16 athletes. So 3-4 is usually where I sit.

Do you guys have regular meetings with the captains group, or is it a by needs basis situation?

I think that this national team with Canada was a little bit more reactive this Summer. There's a lot of factors there. Namely, I was moving countries and started probably the next day. So I think the Summer was a little bit reactive and a little bit ad hoc on how we ran the leadership and understanding like how B team fit into the A team space. This was the very first year we brought a B team in and we carded more athletes than ever before, working with more athletes than ever before. So how the A and B team worked together, it was all a work in progress this year. I think that it will be very different this Summer and next Summer with what that will look like.

But start off regularly. If I was in Australia, it would be a regular meeting. And also at the end of every tour. I like to do a review with staff and players. That would be your leadership group sitting down, "What worked well? What didn't work well? What can we really improve on? Were there any issues? What are some of the strategies we come across?" And if there was ever – as needed as well – if there's something that comes up...

One time in Australia, we at the last minute went to a challenger cup because Kazakhstan couldn't get a visa. We were trying to get a group – a national team – to Peru in less than four days. I need the help from players. That's an as-needed situation.

So yeah, both, I would say.

You were just talking about how you select players or Next Gen B team, A team, and that they're carded. So carded means what they get?

Yeah. The government actually gives them… It's like a salary. Carded just means that they are receiving a monthly income.

How do you keep players motivated or handling the fact that they might be dropping from the A team to the B team, or if they're being carded differently? I assume there's a different salary as well?

Yeah there is. There is a difference.

How is that handled? And I guess, you being the B team coach that falls back on you a little bit as well?

I start off by saying I'm one of the luckiest coaches in the program because I coach the B team. So you know who I coach? I coach the A team players who aren't getting a lot of court time. And I get the young players who are trying to get into the A team. So they are fiery and they are competitive and they're the underdog. That's the best. I'm in the best place to coach. But I would say the one difference between being… I've never, obviously coached professionally in Europe, but I'm assuming there's a big difference between playing for your national team and playing for a club. The motivation, just playing for your country is there already. So athletes know if you want to play for your country, this is what it looks like.

I think if you remove that component from it, I think that the big thing with me is being honest with players about where they're at and where they need to get to. Setting those really clear expectations. I think if you're honest with the player, and you see a path for a player, and you are a resource for that player to get to that end goal, then I think #1 they start to trust you. They're willing to work towards it because they can see the plan. They can see you're part of it. They can see what you're doing to be part of it. But I also think there's this assumption that players don't want to learn. I think a lot of players really want to learn and get technically better. If they're able to learn from you, and they're coming to training, know that you're going to value them, and that you're going to put time and effort into their development, I think that's a huge motivator. At least that they're going to show up every day just wanting to get better.

What's your role in terms of selecting what group of athletes goes to the A team, what's in the B team and then the rest of the programs. Where do you sit and what's your role within that?

For the National Excellence Program, which is the young kids coming through, I run all the identification camps. I'm the only person who sees the athletes. However, we have a selection panel made up of a High Performance director, a national team head coach, junior national team head coach, a Pathways director. I'm part of that selection panel, but I'd say that I'm weighed pretty heavily in there. For our senior national team, last Summer we had a large open trial of... I think there was 70 or 80 people that we could actually fit in our gym, so we cut off at that. If we had to cut it off less than that, we reviewed their videos and decided whether or not it was a good idea for them to be at trials, just so they weren't wasting their trial fee.

During that process we get a lot of coaches in the gym, and they're running the trial. Tom [Black, the national team head coach], myself, and the other coaches from the national team, we're not actually running the trial. We're really walking around, overseeing it, doing an evaluation. A lot of the evaluation is done statistically, so obviously we're taking a lot of numbers. Then the selection of the national team, Tom's like, "These are the ones that I definitely want." These are the ones that are definitely in the A team. Then it's a conversation with the B team, and he's like, "These are the ones who I really think would be good for the B team." Tom obviously has a huge say in who's playing in the B team, but it is a conversation over part of those athletes.

It's really a collaboration amongst the coaches. The way we share opinions and talk about athletes, it's not one person. It's very much a panel. I don't know if that even answers your question. It's a group decision, I guess. But when the athletes are in the B team... And then we had our setter for the B team. She stayed with us for half the Summer, then halfway through she moved up to the A team. Now she's a starting setter with the national A team. She actually was a starting setter for, is it Dresden who won the German cup?

Yep.

She actually started with the B team this Summer and spent two months with us.

So those conversations happen daily. I'm the pain in Tom's butt. And he'd laugh if he heard me say that. I'm always sending him video, and I'm always keeping in the loop, "Hey, this player is doing this," or, "This is where we're at." And then, if there's an opening, or if they're thinking about switching a player out, then that conversation's had. But it's really just about effective communication. Not too hard, right?

Not at all.

So are most all of your A team players and a bunch of your B team players playing professionally?

Yeah.

So you have them then for maximum four months of the year – probably a little less. You have girls over in Europe, and let's be honest, you never know what's going to happen in Europe. How do you kind

of manage that when players come back, maybe doing different technical things?

That's a hard one. I think Tom is really, really particular on what he wants technically, and has a really clear vision for our national team. So obviously I can't speak for him, but I imagine he would be wanting our players to go to clubs who are either closely aligned with that vision, or at least open to different techniques and open to what we're teaching the athletes. We do have a lot of conversations with athletes. Or at least I know from a B team, because our B team athletes tend to go to... They're usually starting out in pro, so they're going to entry-level leagues or entry-level clubs, and they probably don't have the push to be able to say, "Actually, this is what I'm doing." But so they do always ask, "Well, how do I handle this?"

I guess from a national team perspective, I'm always intrigued. If a pro coach is looking at a highlights video and looking at footage and seeing an athlete doing pivot setting, for instance – that seems to be a real topic of debate – and you recruited them, well you recruited them knowing that they're a pivot setter. So why are you trying to change that? I guess that's kind of one of those things that I struggled with personally. But we would encourage athletes going to clubs and coaches who are open to a wide variety of techniques.

I think for us coming back to the national team, we also have to understand that we need athletes to be employed and they need to be employable. So they've got to be able to adapt and they've got to be able to understand in which environment what can they get away with and what do they need to change. I think it's a real balance. It's one that has to be managed from player to player. I think all we do is help provide advice and guidance in it. It's up to the athlete to really manage that relationship. It's a tricky one. It really is.

Yeah, it is.

You talked about sort of managing them when they come back. They can be in any shape possible after their season. What do you find to be your responsibility as a national team coach? You guys are fighting for 2024, but you're also developing an individual athlete, so where do you find your responsibility lies there?

I think number one, our responsibility is to look after the athlete in the way that they can definitely have a successful pro career. I think that that's their livelihood and if they're not fit enough or healthy enough to continue on playing pro throughout the year, they lose their livelihood. Essentially they stop developing at the level we need them to develop at to play in the national team. So I take it very seriously. My job is to keep an athlete healthy throughout the Summer. We do a lot of work around load management where we're informed through science and research. We work with a great IST [Integrated Support Team] around managing athletes' loads. Even though it's college in NCAA as well, like we want them to go back and have good seasons and have successful seasons and be healthy.

I see that as a hundred percent our responsibility, but I also think that we need to do a good job of not managing them throughout the year, but monitoring them. So regular check-ins of how they're feeling mentally, physically. Where we can, we offer resources throughout the year, but it's more to know what we're going to be dealing with come May so that we can plan for that. And we can put plans in place to look after an athlete or to work with an athlete in a way that's safe for them and healthy for them.

If you don't know what to expect come May [start of national team camp] with an athlete – whether they're coming back with niggling injuries, or maybe they're not in a good head space – if you don't actually know where they're at, then I think that's a higher level of risk. So we need to do our best to monitor them throughout the year so we're really clear on where they're at in May, so we can put our plans in place that keeps everyone safe and healthy. And then I really do think it's our job to keep them safe and healthy all year long. So they can go back to their clubs in a good place.

So it's a trade-off for both things?

For sure.

And we don't rely on the clubs to give us information or anything like that at this stage. It's more like we have programs in place where an athlete will fill out a survey. It's just like a wellness survey of where they're at mentally, physically, is there any soreness? We obviously have our IST team, our trainer and our physio who are available year-round to provide advice if needed. We have an S&C staff who are there to supplement a program. Some clubs don't have strength and conditioning coaches at the entry level, so do we need to supplement their program? We have those resources available to us. We want to make sure that our national team program is seen as a 12-month program. It just you're spending eight months of those 12 months with another entity, another program, another college or university. So how do we monitor you best that we're making really informed decisions come May, all the way through to September to keep you safe and healthy and have a long career?

Since you've coached national teams, you generally have one nationality rather than the mix you get in other places. What was it like as a Canadian coaching a group of Australian players?

I don't think I thought it was that different until I came back to Canada and realized my sarcasm and my language kind of gets me in trouble in Canada, whereas that's just the way it is in Australia. Everybody just jokes. They take it seriously, but the things you can get away with saying, and the sarcasm... I kind of miss that. Here, they probably just look at me like, "Oh my God! Does she really mean that?" So I think there's a real "She'll be all right" aspect to Australia. And I love that they're very solutions focused.

In the women's national team, we didn't have a huge budget. It was really tough – like really tough. It was tough for athletes. It was tough for coaches. It was a lot of what we could achieve and the resources we could access were relationship-based, based on what relationships we were able to build with people who are willing to give back to the program. And that was a lot of hard work, but also really rewarding. It was very solutions focused. I think that as much as it was hard, it really set me up to come to Canada and go, "How can we get this done?"

Going with a B team with... Obviously, our program's pretty well-funded, but our B team doesn't get the priority of funding. So it's me like, "Okay, how do I get this done?" And in Australia... You remember us coaching. There was two of us traveling with a manager and a physio. You and I had to take on a ton of different roles. That has set me up to be a more well-rounded coach and then to come into Canada and go, "Okay, we can get this done. We can do this and you can do that." I think that solutions focused mentality of Australia has really helped me.

The Australian national team is generally made up of really not a lot of professional players whereas in Canada the national team is based on professional players. Did you find a difference in the mentality in terms of their professionalism towards their training or their work ethic and that kind of stuff?

I think that back when I was coaching Australia we did have a higher number of professional athletes, so I think that it was a bit easier for me than what Marty [Martin Collins] might have to handle now. But I think there is a difference. I think there's a difference in expectation. I think that I'm held to a higher level of accountability as a coach in Canada. They expect more from me, which is awesome and challenging and frightening, and I'm growing, and learning at a far faster rate than I have ever been. So it's awesome, but that is challenging.

I also think the level of expectation is higher here as well. As a professional athlete they don't have to balance additional work. Some of it is situational in Australia, where they had to balance everything else – study and full-time work, as well as playing for the national team. Here they can only focus on volleyball.

But whether it's situational or not, I feel like I don't have conversations about the sacrifices you have to make. That's just understanding. It's like, "Well, this is my career. This is the career path I've chosen." There's that mentality of, "Well, I'm a professional athlete so of course, I'm going to look after my body. I want to have a long career. Of course I'm going to do the things I need to manage my body and eat right." I think that that was a far sharper learning curve in Australia. I think we got there for a lot of athletes, but for other athletes I think it was still a challenge, for whatever reason. I think it can be a challenge, because of the mentality changes. And I think you can also... When it's someone's livelihood and their actual chosen career path I think that you can have different level of expectation as well.

I don't think my expectations ever changed. I just think that because my expectations didn't change it created a little bit more conflict between the part-time player mentality and what I was expecting because it didn't change. Whether you're a professional or a part-time player, I expected the same out of you.

I look back now and I don't know if I would've changed my expectations at all, but maybe I would have changed my tact and how I presented those expectations. I think that it's something I think I've gotten better at over the years – my tact. As I said, I am blunt. I am honest. But I have to manage perception a little bit. I think I look back and I could have been... Because I understood their pressures. I really did. I understood they were working, they were studying. I think the Australian athletes are really resilient. They have to manage a lot, and so I was understanding of it, but unwavering. I think I could have handled that a little bit differently.

We have a lot of roles as a coach when you're running programs, but do you think there is one quality that's more important than the other, if we're talking about technical, personal communication, tactical, and that kind of stuff?

Obviously, as I've said before, I am a relationships-based coach. I think the ability to build relationships and work with people is for me, the number one quality, but I don't think you can have one without the other. If you don't have the technical or tactical knowledge, people aren't going to buy in. You need to be able to build relationships with people, and understand people, and work with people, and be personable. But if you don't have the technical and tactical knowledge, then it doesn't matter. So you need to have it all.

I think as a young coach I used to get so frustrated with people who always said I was passionate. I was like, "I'm not passionate. I'm knowledgeable." And I used to get so frustrated thinking that because they thought I was passionate they didn't think I was knowledgeable. Now I'm older, and wiser and go, "You don't have to replace one for the other. You can be both. Just because someone said I'm passionate, it doesn't mean they're saying I'm not knowledgeable. You can be both." I actually think you do have to be both. I think you have to, like I said, have good relationships with people. You have to be able to have good relationships with staff and athletes. But if you don't have the technical and tactical knowledge, no one's going to trust you. No one's going to work with you.

Volleyball-wise, how do you weigh the importance of your coaching in preparation compared to match coaching? Is one more important, and why?

One of my favorite quotes is, "Give me six hours to chop down a tree and I'll spend the first four sharpening the ax." I think preparation is key. I think that's where we do most of our learning. Well, that's where we do all of our learning. I think in a game, we can have some influence tactically, we can have zero influence technically, and we can have a lot of influence emotionally. I would say they're both important, but preparation is probably the more important of it.

I think preparation, from not just a tactical or technical standpoint, but even as coaches, having your plan, A, B, C, D, E, F, G, having a strategy for your timeouts, having a strategy for your subs, having a strategy for how your staff are going to work and making sure everybody's aware of that. I think preparation is key, and that's something I think I've gotten a lot better at over the years.

Professionally, I would agree. But professionally we get judged quite a lot on what's happening in the particular match. "Did you take a time out? Why didn't you take a time out?" Almost like the match coaching is more important for the management to see you doing something. Is that something that you find to be the case in national programs, or is it a little more hands-off in terms of that kind of situation?

I think they're a little bit more hands-off. This will probably, at some stage, lead into some of the gender questions you want to go through. I do think that we're really quick to have really strong opinions on female coaches. I think we have to prove that we can coach, where men have to prove they can't coach. That's probably a really strong statement that might get me into trouble, but I do find that people are really quick to offer me their opinion, whether that's peers, or club coaches, provincial team coaches, state team coaches.

I found it more so in Australia than in Canada, but a lot of opinions on strategies. Not knowing the why's, just judging the what's. I think the reality is that coaches get far too much credit for wins and losses in the moment. My job as a coach, I think, is to prepare a team and then do my best to stay out of their way in a game. I just think that we don't get as much from the national league.

Our federations have always been pretty supportive. I don't think we deal with the same level of management and administration that you guys do at the pro club level. From the general public, I have found that they are more... Not so much in Canada. Like I said, I've been here a year. But more so in Australia, they were really willing to offer their opinions a lot, and some were really, really valuable and others – as one of my mentors would say – is white noise.

All right. What would a typical international season look like? Are there phases to it? Can you talk me through that?

That is a really tough question because you're really bound by the competitions you have on that Summer. This Summer we expected there to be the Olympics, which we didn't qualify for. It was a really heavy B Team focused Summer. The A Team would have VNL. Then we have Pennant Cup at the end of Summer that may be a mixture, but the B Team had quite a few competitions – not FIVB competitions – but competitions throughout the Summer. How we manage that... A lot of how I manage is what I learned from Australia around load management. Load management is a huge part in Australia.

Honestly, one of my biggest learning curves was around load management. That really informed when we take breaks, or how we're going to manage those breaks. We want to make sure that athletes go back to their pro or their college season also well-rested in a good frame of mind. If we can give an athlete a break for some time in the summer, we will. We just have to manage it well. The breaks that we take are really based on what competitions we have on. If Vienna had gone ahead in May, we would've had a really short lead-in-time because athletes would come back from their pro clubs and then it would be really quick lead-in-time.

Whereas last year we had the challenger cup to get into VNL, which was later. We had quite a long preparation phase, and then we took our breaks later in the Summer. It really just depends on what we have on. I know for me as a coach we are really driven by the information we get from load management principles and obviously, our IST staff.

I have a few questions about that. In terms of technology – the load monitoring you were talking about – how would you guys implement that? Were you using anything like GPS's or VERT's? How did you implement and that? (For those who don't know, Australia is a country that is one of the leading countries in sports science. Shannon was working at the then – I think it's still called – the Australian Institute

of Sport, and they're some of the leading sports scientists and people there. She has a pretty good knowledge on this stuff.)

We use VERT's to count our jumps or our external loading. We look at the number of jumps an athlete is doing every day across a week. But we also look at internal loading and we use a system with the AIS called Athlete Management System, where an athlete can input their general wellness. How much sleep they're getting, how they're feeling, their energy levels, any soreness. They also then record the length of a session and what their rate of perceived exhaustion is. I'm not going to give you a course in load management, but that gives you essentially a figure of how they rate the day. Then you look at what their average is over four weeks. Then you want to keep your acute load – your seven day load – within an 80% to 130% [of the 4-week average] to minimize risk of injury.

We use a VERT, and we use a scale. It's a subjective scale, but considering it's the same athlete scaling every single day, it's consistent. We also do regular physical testing. This something that we obviously use a little bit. If we see across the board that everyone's really low on their jump testing, then we know maybe they're just feeling a little bit low and maybe are ready for a break. That information then informs when we take a break. Can we afford to take a break, or are we going to go into a trough? Are we going to drop below that load for the week, and that's going to put them at risk when they come back to full training? Maybe we need to shorten the amount we're training for the end of the week because we're already really high.

It also gives you this concept of how to build up an athlete for a season. This is why I look at some programs. I'm not sure from where you sit, but I know I look at some of these college programs and they run these huge pre-seasons. They just kill them. I always wonder, "Hey, I'm all for just working an athlete hard, but how did they prepare the athlete and the athlete's body to withstand that because your most important part is your season?"

We know that if you have a massive spike in loads, you're at risk of injury over the next four weeks, right? If you do the spike in pre-season, they could have a really high rate of injury or high risk of injury at the start of the season. I always wonder that sort of thing. I've gone on a tangent, sorry. I hope that's the question.

Load management is more effective done all year round. Do you guys take loads from players professionally?

In Australia, we didn't. We aimed to do it. I'm not sure why we didn't. We try to do about 4-6 weeks out. We start to get a feel, get their numbers in. What they are doing, how often they're doing it, what was their Rate of Perceived Exhaustion, so we have a baseline of where they're at. We also had the full-time program then, so half of our team was with me anyways. I was already able to track their loads through the Athlete Management System.

With Canada, we would definitely get an idea if their loads fed back into the program. But it's not all year long because we can't do anything about their loads when they're in pro [season]. If they're going to have a spike or a trough, that's really on their coach. What we need to know is where they're at when they come back to us. So that 4-6 weeks before they come back to us we want to know where they're at.

At first as a coach, I was more of the mindset, "Well, don't tell me how to coach. What do you mean this figure is going to tell me how to coach?" I realized it's actually not about load management telling me how to coach, or dictating the decisions I make. Load management just helps you make informed decisions, coming up with plans. If I know that an athlete coming into the season only has about 800 jumps for the week, well, I'm not going to all of a sudden plan a program that has barely any jumping, or a plan that has 2,000 jumps.

It's just making informed decisions. For me to make informed decisions, I need to have the information available to me.

You mentioned something about with the Canadian athletes, the wellness check-in. Are you guys doing something like that? What questions would be on that?

Yeah, the wellness check-in has only just been put into place over the last, I think it was literally last week. We're using a new program that it sends them a reminder. It's a link to a survey and the survey will be questions around... I haven't actually looked at the survey yet because it only came out last week, but the questions will be around how much sleep are they getting, the quality of sleep, any soreness? I believe there's usually energy levels. Australia had one as well – energy levels, and they could highlight the areas in their body that were sore, or that sort of thing.

What do you do if a player's reporting low sleep? I guess you don't want to use these check-ins to police them, but obviously it's very important to sleep. How would you handle that if you see someone's just really not doing very well?

Yeah, we would get a notification if they were sleeping less than a certain amount. But because I have the benefit of working with IST staff, I feel like there're some conversations that are best for them to have. Just like even things around mental health or that sort of thing. I'm part of it. I definitely know what's going on, but that's their area of specialty. They can relate back to an athlete, how sleep can impact their performance, and how it can impact how well they learn. And they can relate that back to what they can do on court. We would get them to have that conversation.

It's not usually they're just refusing to sleep. There could be some underlying things there. Maybe they are struggling with other aspects. Then we can refer them to other resources in our team as well, so we have that benefit.

I think about things like nutrition. If we feel like an athlete's nutrition is of question, we would have our dietician – nutritionists in Australia – speak to the athlete. I feel like sometimes as coaches we try and do everything ourselves and it's actually really good to let someone, whose expertise is in that area, speak to the athlete.

Between maybe the Australian program and the Canadian program, is there anything else technology-wise that you guys use that stands out?

We use different technologies. All the study we do on like velocity versus accuracy and serve. Obviously, we use our radar guns for serving. I would say in Canada, Tom is a real fan. We use a lot of video – live video – in training. We always have TVs on the side of the court so athletes can see themselves.

On a delay?

Yeah, on a video delay. He uses Apple TV. When I'm by myself I use the BAM – BUST-A-MOVE – app. I also use Coach's Eye when I want to stop the video and draw lines and stuff. We always have video up in our gym during the learning phases of training. We don't use it as much during… Tom always has it up on 6-on-6 so athletes can have a look, but I usually take mine down in 6-on-6. I'm usually just using it in the learning part of training.

We use VolleyMetrics with our national team in Canada. We didn't have access to that in Australia and I thought that was a major disadvantage. Not only can you see your opponents, but you can learn from other teams, and you really have at hand any footage you want.

That's the thing is I want to look at with NCAA athletes coming through to Next Gen. I watched all their footage. I've seen these players play a ton and that is a huge advantage for me as a coach. I think it's also really powerful to be able to approach a player and say, "Hey, I want to see you at trials. I caught that game that you played against so-and-so and wow! You did a good job there." Or the players, who go back to college here in the national team. I have conversations with them, "Hey, I really want to see you work on that first step." You can have really good conversations with them.

We used video and stuff a lot in Australia. Just probably not as much as I am using in Canada now.

I can't think of anything else really. Having a scout at training has been awesome. [Here Shannon is both referring to a person and a statistical report produced by that person.] I don't get it as much. Tom gets it every day, but I get it sometimes. I never got it in Australia because all of our scouts were international so we've got them for competitions only. That's huge, though, and that's something I would love to see. I'd love a scout every single day at training.

You mentioned when you guys are doing the tryouts a lot of the evaluations are statistical. Is there some threshold that you're wanting to reach? Are you comparing them against each other in those trials outs, or what?

I think the obvious position is a libero. I think that we need to make sure that each athlete is getting at least 300 balls. We've got to make sure the sample size is big enough. That was actually a real challenge at trials – making sure the liberos that were there were getting the numbers they needed for the stats to be relevant. We would want them to be at least passing 300 balls, and then we could compare them.

To be honest, it was all comparative because it's all relative to the level. Trials are obviously not as high of a level as our Senior A National Team. They're at trials, but the levels isn't as high, so it's relative. We use it more as comparative, but it's probably most important for our liberos.

Switching topics a little… In Australia, you coached in a league where it's week-to-week games. You've coached the national team. Now, you're coaching nationally, but also running a development program at the same time. What are your favorite parts of coaching?

I do love coaching international volleyball. I love coaching the Senior National Teams. I think you're working with these exceptional athletes, who can do exceptional things, and if you can find ways to get even one or two percent better, than that's a huge challenge. I think that's exciting. I love the tactics of the international game, the speed, the multi-zone offense, and having the players with the ability to play at that level. That's exciting. I love that.

But it's also equally rewarding working with development players. I haven't been in the trenches like a lot of the coaches. The young 17-, 18-year-olds I work with are the best in the country. That's pretty good.

As much as I love working with development athletes – and it's rewarding because their rate of progression and their rate of improvement is so fast – I think there's just a real art of coaching with international volleyball. How to find those little percentages to get better with athletes and as a team. Doing gap analysis about what are the best teams doing? How far back are we from them and how can we close that gap? How is our development team helping us close that gap in the future years?

I do love it all, but my favorite thing is definitely the athletes, 100%.

What keeps you motivated to coach? It is one of the tougher careers, especially family-wise. What are some ongoing motivations for you?

I haven't given this a lot of thought. It's something that I'm really passionate about. I love to do it, and so it never feels like work to me. I'm always excited about it. I think that's so rare to be able to do something that you love so much. For me, that's why I keep doing it.

I also find my ego tells me to have an impact on that many people, and to be working with athletes to help them achieve their own goals. My ego loves that too – to know that I was a part of someone's journey, and to have a positive impact on someone. I think that my ego loves that.

It's not as if you've been coaching since you were a little kid, or even since you were finished really playing seriously. What was your job?

Oh, I worked in community development. So I did a post-grad in community development. I used to work with migrant and refugee families and it was about connecting them to the community and helping them grow and thrive in our community in Australia. So I guess there's always been a part of me that's wanted to help.

I just find it really interesting because you talk to a lot of high level coaches, and they basically just switched straight from playing to jump into coaching. Or they grew up coaching, like in your town school – something like that. But you have a job that probably honestly pays better than ones that you have now, and you choose to coach. There's not a lot of people that make that choice.

Yeah, no, I just love it. I loved what I did before, but it was still work. It didn't consume me. I'm not saying it consumes me in a negative way, but there's not a day that goes by that I don't think of coaching. I think I'm in a space right now where I'm so excited for where a team kind of can get to. And I really believe that 2024 is a possibility, and 2028, and I can be a part of building something awesome. We've done a good job here, but there's so much more work to do. There's a lot of it that there is a blank slate and I get to be part of creating something and developing something. That's pretty cool. Yeah. I love it.

What are some sort of mistakes you've made in your coaching career and things you've learned from them? Do you have any examples?

I mean, you can probably identify with this – meaning you were part of it. I sucked at managing staff. I'm a lot better at it now, but I've still got work to do. When I first started coaching, I wanted to do everything myself. It wasn't that I didn't trust people. It's that I almost felt pressure to show I knew everything. You know what I mean? And so I didn't want to let go of some of the tasks or some of the responsibility. What I realized through that is I wasn't working people and getting the most out of people. They stuck with me, but did they feel like they were a valuable contribution? I don't know. Not early on, probably not. They probably thought they were part of *my* plan rather than a part of *our* plan. I think that's something I've gotten better at – kind of bringing people along for the journey and really trusting people in the roles that they play. Knowing that this is our journey, it's not my journey. And really trying to show how much I value staff and gain the most out of them.

I think I've been better also... Early on I probably was afraid to admit to people that I didn't know things, or that I wasn't very good at something. When you don't do that, then you don't really recognize your gaps and you kind of ignore your gaps. So I wasn't necessarily getting the most people to fill those gaps. I don't think I was the best. I'm not the best now, but I don't know if that even makes sense. I feel like I rambled, but staff management every year is something I want to get better and better and better at. I think I'm getting better every year, but I still think I have a long way to go.

Anything else you want to add, or any thoughts?

I just think that it wasn't until I stepped into other roles I realized I need to be better at it. I've always been a head coach. It wasn't until this year that I stepped into an assistant coaching role and was like, "Oh, so that's what my assistant coaches were complaining about." I really think that I had to see it from their perspective. And I think some people have this awesome ability to do that without actually stepping into their shoes. But for me, I stepped into the shoes. I already knew some of it, but I stepped into the shoes and really it really hit home with me how important those small things are, how much better I have to be at certain things.

Changing topics, what was your motivation to be part of this Wizard Women series?

I don't think my reasons very far from yours. I think that we always say you can't be what you can't see, and I don't think that there are enough visible role models out there for women coaches. If this helps raise the profile of women coaches and the awesome things that they're doing, and it inspires other women to get involved or coach – even if it's at a club level or a university level or a pro level, whatever – if this helps, then I'm all in for sure.

I can speak for Europe and in the national team scene. I can't speak too much for NCAA, but women are pretty underrepresented in coaching, at least professionally and in the national teams. What are some of the barriers that you think that we face as coaches and why we're under represented?

I think there's a range of factors. I think there's practical factors, there's personal ones, and there's the socio-cultural ones. I think that women have different roles in a family unit, whatever their family unit might look like. I think that we historically have a very different role, and with that comes different pressures and different needs. The coaching model and the support systems around it are set up for men who have different needs, different roles in society, so the support isn't always there for women. I think without visible role models, we don't necessarily see it as a viable career path. We don't aspire to be someone because we don't see them.

I also think there's a lot of unintentional bias that we even hold as women. I was mostly coached by men, so I automatically thought men were probably better coaches.

I also think a lot of our... I don't know about pro in Europe, but I know with high-performance directors, most of them are men. We do hire like, whether we intend to, or realize it, or not. We identify with with people who are more similar to us.

I think those are some of the barriers. There's a lot more. I think it's a range for each person as well. Some might go, "Oh, I really identify with that. Yeah. I really noticed that." And others may actually... Actually that wasn't true for me, but maybe this one's true for me. I think there's just such a wide range of barriers for women coaching.

You mentioned really early on a couple of your coaching influences, and you sort of mentioned they were mentors as well. Is there any-

thing else that's been able to support you specifically being a female in this journey?

I think having your support system, professionally and personally. I think for me, with kids, it was really important that my husband was supportive of my career path and knew what I wanted to do, because I think there is a lot of strain that that puts on relationships. I think that's for coaches across the board. Our significant other, no matter of our gender, is under a lot of strain. I think that our relationships were put under that. So making sure you have a person who is supportive is really important.

I think that some of the best advice I got when I first started coaching was when I voiced my needs. I said, "Well, no one's hearing me." And they say, "You haven't found your person yet." So you'll eventually find your person professionally who's going to support you as a mentor, or support you just in your development path. Keep looking for that person because you will eventually find them. If I had just stopped at the one or two that I realized weren't on the same page as me, or weren't as invested in my development as I had hoped, then I probably wouldn't be where I am. But I kept looking for someone who was going to be really invested in my development.

Have there been any challenges that you've faced that would be unique to a female coach?

I mean, there're the ones that don't actually impact things. Sometimes you get sexual remarks and sometimes you get the referees handing the... I actually get that a lot – handing the lineup card to someone else. Or you get "Where's the coach?" Or they assume you're the trainer. But I mean at the end of the day, that's on them. That doesn't really impact our job going forward.

I think one of the challenges I realized early on... Once I got into high performance coaching, I was like, "Finally, I have a seat at the table." But it's really different between having a seat at the table and having a voice at the table. That's why I think it's important to find your person who's going to professionally back you. Maybe it's not a mentor. Maybe it's someone within your club or your organization who, when you get around the table and you have an idea, they're going to be on board with you being heard.

Early on I desperately just wanted to be seen as the same as my peers. I didn't want to ask for special support or ask for special consideration because I wanted to be seen as an equal. So early on I think I sacrificed a lot personally with my family. Looking back, I didn't need to do that. I just... I didn't have the confidence to ask for the things I needed. I almost needed someone to go, "Hey, have you thought about asking her if she needs this? And have you thought about asking her if she might need that?" It sounds ridiculous because I was a head coach of a national team, but I almost needed someone to go, "Have you thought about her and her needs yet?"

So now I ensure that – and I am grateful now in Canada I do have those people around me – but I make sure I try and be that voice for other women. "Have you thought that maybe she shouldn't be asked to give up her whole day, right before she goes on a 5-week tour, because she's going to miss her children." Not that that happened. That was just a random example. But I just think early on that I didn't feel confident in asking for the things I needed. And it's also unrealistic to think that other people know what you need. So it's just this horrible relationship where I want you to know what I need, but I'm afraid to tell you what I need, because I want to be seen as the same, but you don't know what I need because, well, you're not me. I found that really challenging.

You mentioned there about the day off. You're a mom of three – which I still can't believe – and a high performance coach. I can't even imagine the challenges that you face there. How good are the current support systems within organizations, and how can they improve?

I think it's tough. I don't think there are a lot of women who coach at the national team level across sports. There aren't a lot of them. I can only speak for the federations I've worked for. And like I said, early on, because

I desperately – and maybe it was my own insecurities – but I desperately wanted to be seen as an equal. I really didn't ask for the things I needed. Afterwards I realized my work-life balance was really terrible, and that wasn't sustainable. So while I thought I did an okay job my first year, I think I survived my first year. So how could I thrive in this environment? I knew that I needed to start asking for the things I needed. And it took a while for me to find people who are going to hear me, and find people who are going to support that.

I'm better at that now. When I came to Canada, I remember I landed by myself with three kids. My husband was still in Australia. I landed on a Thursday. Our first trial with the national team was on the Monday, but it was the day that my kids were going to start school. Well two of them, because one is too young. But they were going to start school in a brand new school. I went straight to Tom, and I was so nervous because I would never have done this previously, but I'm like, "Nope, you need to ask what things you want." I said, "Tom," I go, "It's my kid's first day of school in a new country. My husband's still in Australia. Can I come to training a bit late?" And he's just like, "Of course." He's like, "Shannon, no question." He's like, "Go do what you need to do for your kids. We got you. We'll see you as soon as you get here, no stress."

And that has honestly been Tom's standpoint on everything this Summer. He was very aware of my situation with my husband in Australia. He was so supportive, and because of his very first reaction to that question I've never hesitated to really voice what I need. That was huge.

I can't say I had that experience in Australia. It wasn't negative, but the first few comments I got were around, "Do you think you can really do this with three kids?" Whether appropriate or not, that then put my thinking around, "Well, I need to prove that I can do it. I need to prove I'm the same. I need to prove that." I think the comment was made really about trying to look out for me, but the way it was made was... It then set the tone for how I operated in Australia. So I do think we can get a lot better for women who coach. I really do. I think we can get a lot better for all coaches with families, not just women, but men as well.

One of the other challenges we really faced in Australia is we didn't have the family support system. We didn't have free daycare and stuff, so you would have your regular daycare from 9 to 5, but most of the coaches work is outside of regular business hours. When I'm in the country, my husband works in a normal job so he could be home at night. But when I leave the country I need more help with that. We had to pay a lot for those extra services. I think that alone would have been a start – helping when we're on long tours, helping with the extra nanny services, and stuff that we need to get.

And I think the hardest part to this day is something – it's not unique to coaches – but the mom's guilt. My four-year-old had a Mother's Day celebration at preschool one year, and I was on tour with... I was actually coaching the U23 team at the time. I had one of my Senior national Team players go with him to his Mother's Day celebration where they did spa. They did nails and stuff. So I have his preschool book where it shows memories, and it has my former player there on Mother's Day taking a picture with them. I felt so guilty about it, but I look back now and no, we got it done.

My parenting normal is very different than someone else's parenting normal, but it's normal for us. It's normal for my kids.

Yeah, absolutely. Get rid of that shame.

Easier said than done, but yeah. We just need to cut ourselves a break a little bit.

If there was one misunderstanding or stereotype of female coaches that you would want to clear up or argue against, what would that be?

That women don't want to coach. Is that a stereotype? I mean, I hear that so often. I hear people say, "Well, why don't women coach?" And they go,"Not as many women want to coach at this level. Not as many women want to coach as a profession." Maybe that's an assumption, but that's not true.

Like I said, there's a lot of barriers to women coaching. The biggest one is that there's not a lot of visible role models. So they don't actually know that's an option careerwise. They don't actually know that's something they can aspire to be.

Then there are other challenges that we faced around the support systems that are tailored to men who coach. And the coaching paradigm has looked a certain way for so long. Until we change what a coach looks like, the support systems won't change. So there are barriers to women coaching, whether we accept them or not. They're different for each woman, but there are barriers.

The other one that drives me nuts is that we're all sensitive, and want to cry. Women are different. Every woman is different. Now, I will say that I am sensitive. I don't cry a ton, but I am sensitive. But not all women are sensitive and they're not criers. And you know what? If I have an emotional moment with the team, and I'm going to let a tear out, then I want to let that tear out. My players know that I'm being authentic. I'm being genuine. I'm being vulnerable. That's what makes me an awesome coach. But it doesn't make me this weak, sensitive person. It just makes me human and being human is what's enabled me to connect with my athletes. So that's another one that drives me mental.

All right. We'll start to wrap this up. So I would like to know if there're any books you can recommend that people could read, or that you loved?

I do love to read. I think that the one I'm reading right now – funnily enough, I think I recommended it to you – is *Women Kind: Unlocking the Power of Women Supporting Women*. That's a cool one that I'm reading right now.

One of my favorite books that I recommend to a lot of people is *Legacy* about the All Blacks. It's obviously around culture.

I'm a fan of *Captain's Class.*

And another one that didn't take me where I thought it would was *Sacred Hoops* by Phil Jackson. That's another good book. That's probably what's on my bedside table right now.

Those books there. And I read a heap of other nonfiction books that have nothing to do with volleyball. I need a break sometimes.

Last question. Do you have any advice for developing coaches or people starting in the profession? It can't be don't have kids. No, I'm kidding.

Oh yeah. Seriously though. I have that conversation with players. Don't worry. It could be a whole generation where there's a gap in young kids. You're like, "Why was Shannon coach though?" No, I'm joking.

Yeah, I think that you need to take charge of your own development, just like we ask athletes to. And read, but go and watch coaches coach. Ask to go in their gyms. Ask them questions. Connect with them online. I'm always so willing to have coaches in my gym, and I'm willing to... I think the other day I got a phone call from a local youth sport coach who just wanted to have a chat on a few things. I've never even met her. It was just an opportunity to share some ideas and share my thoughts on things. Coaches are really willing to share. That's an awesome part about our profession. It is such an open sport.

I think that how I developed the quickest was when I was willing to put myself out there and ask questions, and ask to go to their trainings and watch their trainings. Then go to games and ask them after, "Okay, well, what were you talking about in that time out? What was your strategy there?" Just really pick their brains.

I think that coaching courses are there for certification, but if you really want to develop as a coach, you need to put yourself out there and connect with other coaches.

Chapter Two

Erin Appleman

Erin Appleman, from the U.S., has been the head coach at Yale University since 2003. In that time her teams have won or shared the Ivy League title 12 times and made 8 trips to the NCAA tournament. The first of those, in 2004, was the first time an Ivy League team reached the second round, which they repeated in 2008. Prior to her time at Yale, she assisted at Penn State, helping them to Big Ten titles and Final Four appearances. In this interview Erin talks about how she changed the culture at Yale and how she recruits. She also shares her thoughts about barriers to female coaching and ideas which could help make coaching a more accessible career option for young mothers.

***

Could you please start telling us about your history and experience in volleyball? How'd you get here? And a little bit about your journey.

Sure. I'm going to go way back. I started in eighth grade, really enjoyed the sport, and played all through high school I played club and ended up going to college, playing volleyball on a volleyball scholarship. Started my first job at USD [University of San Diego]. My assistant at my school got the head job there and he insisted, so I started there. Did that, went to night school, and worked a paying job, so I had three things I was doing at once.

Kind of crazy. I was earning around $5,000 for the year, so it was more like an internship. And then a year later I said, "I really want to see if this is what I want to do with my life," and got rid of the job that gave me money, and just went and did it all day. Instead of just being a practice coach I was able to get to see the back scenes – see how recruiting worked, and scheduling, and budgets, and all of that.

I went from USD to [California State] Northridge for a year, and then got really lucky and ended up at Penn State. I was at Penn State for about nine, ten years. We went to five Final Fours, and won a national championship in '99. So I was really fortunate there. And then I actually had my second child, and decided to be an at-home mom for a couple of years. Then my husband got transferred to... He's also a coach, so he then went to a place in Rhode Island. Looking for a job, I found Yale. I've been here for 18 years. It kind of fell into my lap, I'll be honest. I'm just so, so fortunate to be at Yale. I really love it.

What are the biggest differences between Penn State and Yale?

I think the biggest difference between being an assistant coach and a head coach is, if you've ever seen those cartoon characters where there's those bubbles of thoughts above you, as an assistant, you might have three or four, and as a head coach you have like 30 all the time. You definitely become more of a manager than just doing a certain job. You're looking after 10 things at once. And I think early on it was pretty overwhelming, I'll be honest. Then, as you start to build your culture – and you have to pick things that work for you – once those start working, then you can broaden what you want to do and what you can accomplish.

Through my years just being at Yale I've seen coaches - new coaches, young coaches – come in and try it different ways, and I really feel the most important thing is to just do five things really well. Then the second year, keep those five and do another four or five. Instead of trying to do all 20 things all in the same year. Just really try to build that culture slowly.

Could you talk about some coaching influences, whether it be initial, or ongoing coaching influences that you have?

Sure. My father played and was my coach for a couple years, so definitely my father. I think the first year he coached me he said, "Go right," I went left. And then the second year… I was young, so he would drive me to and from practices about an hour away. So we'd be in the car together for a long time and I started realizing that he knew what he was talking about, and started really paying attention. I was a setter, so the quarterback of the team. Having a coach talk to me all the time really helped me understand how to be a leader, and how to direct traffic, and how to be a good setter, which I think has helped in the coaching as well.

And then Mollie Kavanagh, who was my club coach, was probably one of the best coaches I've ever been a part of. She really believed that, as many touches as you possibly could have in a practice is the best thing. So it was a very fast paced practice. A lot of touches, it wasn't one ball and six people, it was one ball, two people. One ball, one person. It was constantly getting multiple touches.

And then, of course, I would have to say Russ Rose from Penn State – arguably one of the best U.S. coaches in the country. He really influenced the way I think. We do a lot of the stuff we did at Penn State. When I was his assistant, I was 23 – really young – and I learned so much from him throughout my career. Just how to manage people, and the relationships that become so much more important. And I don't think I understood that early on, as a young coach, that the relationships is really the most important thing.

Just a small question from that. You said you were a setter. I've noticed there's a lot of coaches that are showing up that were setters when they were players. I was also, actually. Do you think there's any special reason for that?

Definitely. We're used to doing... On the court, you're calling plays, you're seeing the blocks on the other side, you're figuring out what the best rotation is, you're moving passers, you're directing traffic the entire time you're playing. So I think that comes pretty natural when you start to be in coaching. You can try to direct traffic and figure out what's really the important thing right now. Is getting the ball to that hitter the most important, or is whatever? You're making those decisions all the time, and as a head coach you rely on those.

How has your coaching philosophy changed over time?

I'm definitely more efficient as a coach. I thought early on it was... I had to expend a lot of energy, and when I was an assistant most of the team relied on my energy and I could pump them up and stuff like that. As I've gotten older, I feel like it's better to be a solid, stable presence - whether we're up, whether we're down, whatever we're doing - so they can always look to me and they don't have to... If I'm mad at them, they're not going to know. They're going to just see me as an even keel, so they can look to me for advice versus energy. And I think that's an important thing for a head coach – just to be calm. And yes, I get excited, and I do fist pumps, and those kind of things. But you still want to have just more... patience, I think is the biggest term. I think honestly having kids really helped me with that, having more patience.

I can imagine that. What about training methodology? Are there a lot of differences between a training session from then to now?

Not really. I always tell my team, I'm kind of a boring coach, I have about ten drills that I like, but they're all super important, and we're going to be really good in these ten things. Our seasons are quick, and I'm not sure you can be great at everything, so I want to be good at a few things. I want to be great at a few things, I should say. So we really practice those things. I've gotten a few more drills along the way, obviously, but at the same time, I don't know if there's really a difference in how I train, other than now I trust more people to train. My first year at Yale I did all the conditioning,

I did all the weight lifting, I did everything. And now we have people and staff that can do that for me. So it's trusting them that they're taking care of things.

How did you begin to trust those people? I know that's difficult as a young coach, to give up control, but how did you make that transition?

I think I'm a pretty good delegator, so I'm pretty good with that. I have my assistant, who's been with me for 17 out of my 18 years. Obviously, I trust him very much. First you have to see what they're doing, and then believe in it, and then let it go, and trust that the players. You've also been building trust with them, so they're going to tell me, "Hey, you know what? This isn't working," or whatever the situation is, "I felt uncomfortable in here," "I'm hurting my back." Then I can maybe go in and talk to those people that are handling the team in certain ways. So it's really just making sure I've got that trust of the players that they can come to me and talk to me.

While we're just on the staff topic a little bit, you've had one assistant who's been there for quite a while. Beyond that, is there a way that you select your staff, and then do you have specific roles for them? How would you set that up among the staff?

Yes, my second assistant has been with me for seven years. Prior to when I was hiring Brendan [her 2nd Assistant from 2014 to 2019] for me it was more of the overall person. When I hired Kevin [her 1st Assistant], I looked at what my strengths were, and what my weaknesses were, and made sure I tried to get someone who could complement me. When I was at Penn State, I recruited all the time. I was a pretty good recruiter, so when I was hiring my first assistant, I didn't need to bring in someone who could recruit. What I needed to do was bring in someone who could train the team while I was out on the road recruiting, in different aspects. For me, it was really important that I found somebody who understood volleyball and got it. And for some great reason we have very similar philosophies on the game. So that has worked out well.

When I hired my second assistant, I was looking to have someone help me a little bit more in recruiting and do some things of that nature. I don't really divide by staff into, "Okay, you have middles and you have passers and you have this." Everybody does a little bit of everything. But my second assistant was a setter, and he trains a lot of our blocking and our middles, and my first assistant was a libero, so he does a lot of defense and passing. It kind of naturally happened that way. But typically we try to have practices where we're just working with one group, so all three of us can work with that group, then the other group comes in, instead of having two courts going in with two different practices.

And I divvy up the responsibilities really according to their strengths. The fact that I think I'm a good recruiter means I'm going to continue to recruit. Just because I became head coach doesn't mean I'm not going to do that. One of the things I did a lot as an assistant was our travel. So for a long time, I still did travel. No other head coach does travel, but for me, travel was a really important aspect, because nothing upsets a team more when all of a sudden we have no food, or we're late to a game. You have to be flexible, but it can become a problem, so you want to make sure that it's done right. For a lot of years I did travel. I've given that to Brendan over the years, but I still look it over all the time. I'm still kind of controlling that part.

How do you talk with the staff and identify their strengths before they come? I know it's not necessarily that simple, and I know you've had quite a long relationship with a couple of the staff, but beforehand how do you find that in each?

I wish I could tell you. I think I got really lucky. I felt comfortable enough with my knowledge and what I wanted to accomplish at Yale that I could just go out and hire someone who I thought could do one or two jobs. Now, obviously, since they've been here, they do a lot more than one or two jobs, but I felt in my first couple of years I had my finger in every aspect, and now I don't have to. But I think I felt comfortable knowing from top to bottom how to run a program, that I just needed people to come in and support that. Now they each could go and run a program, no doubt.

You pretty much came into Yale and turned the program around after you arrived. You talked about focusing on five things that you want to be great at. What were some keys that you focused on when you arrived, that you thought would get the success that you have got?

I took over a program where the coach had been fired, and I think that for me it was just trying to find that win again, that passion for volleyball. Very quickly it became apparent that they just did it because they felt like they had to. So for me it was having them find their passion and their love of the game again, then convincing them to win. I can remember one of my first road trips we went to a university and we were better than the team, and we lost. I remember saying to the team in the locker room, "Why? Why did we lose?" And they were like, "Well, we've never won here." And I remember saying to them, "I've never lost here. I want to win." And so I think changing that culture of expectations, to win, to find the love... The hard work comes because you love it. And I think in my first couple of years, it was a lot of training, a lot of... Learning volleyball IQ I think was one of the big ones.

So there was a couple things I really wanted to focus on. It was the passion, learning the volleyball IQ, and teaching them to win. So we competed every day in practice. We did something, if not multiple things, of competition to get them back into that, "Hey, it's not just drills. It's you have to find a way to win." And then I was able to recruit people that could win. My first couple of years, I would recruit players that maybe weren't stars on a winning program, but were on a winning program, versus a star on a team that didn't win. For me, it was more important to find those people that knew how to win or were around people that won a lot. Then I could get them to start to believe. Now we can recruit those players who are stars on those winning teams.

But it takes a process, so you have to start from the beginning and find out, what does your program need? If you need to find a way to win, and maybe finding the best players that maybe lose isn't the answer. Finding the players that maybe are a sub or a role player on a team that wins, maybe they'll step up and they can teach someone else how to win, which was what I wanted to do.

So the main focus was getting players in that know how to compete, and then getting them competing every single day.

Yeah. Who could pepper the longest? Who could do this the longest? Anything we did, there was some sort of competition. And I don't really do a ton of punishment if you lose, because to me that just wastes a lot of time in practice. When this team would win, I would take one of the good players out, put another player on. Can you do it again? So for me it was more of just pushing them to believe they could win at the end of the day.

That ties into the next thing I wanted to ask about. You've obviously created a winning culture, and we talked a little bit about how you developed that, but is there anything specific that you would want to touch on about having a winning culture?

Yeah. I think early on we just competed a lot. We worked on winning. I was able to get good recruits, which got me better recruits, which got me better recruits. But along the way I also came up with some core values for our program. I didn't have these when I first got here. It was probably ten years ago, so I was about halfway through. We came up with some core values of our team that talks about our culture, and it's a hand.

It's the pinkie process. It's processing – whether that's watching video, processing what I'm telling you, doing the your lifting. Unity is your ring finger, so knowing that we're a unit and we have to be able to get along – especially on the court – that we're all working for a good goal. The middle finger would be the competitiveness. That's self-explanatory. Then there's a drive. A lot of the cars right now, you push a button to drive the car, so your index finger was drive. Do you have the drive to work hard every day, in the weight room, off-season, those kind of things? And then the last one which was important to me was your thumb up, which is fun. I wanted to have fun. To me, I want to laugh in practice. There's always something funny. Someone trips or someone gets hit in the face. Something funny happens, and you want to be able to have a culture that allows that. And I think the team really enjoys those aspects.

So those are our five core values of the Yale volleyball program. We recruit with those, we talk about it with our recruits, we talk about it with our team, all the time. Unity, who have you reached out today to make sure they're okay? Or can we be competitive today? Hey, this is a hard drill. You've got to have drive to finish it strong. Things of that nature. I've changed some of my language to fit the culture as well, but to me that was a really big step that got us this direction, was figuring it out. And I think not everybody should have the same core values, but finding them, and what's important to you... I've been here for so long that they're ours, but I hope if I leave that they still stay with the program.

So that's an every day thing for you then. These five values, they're coming out your mouth all the time.

Yeah, and it took a while, because I don't really use some of those words, so it took a while to think about process in a way I could say it during practice. That wasn't a word I really used that much in coaching. It was more like, "Hey, learn it this way, or do this," and now it's like, "Hey, the process is this." So it took a while to get there. And you talk about it being the same. I think that was the really important part of it, because I think there's teams that have... Okay, this is the theme of the year, which I think is also important. And we still do that. We still have a logo of the year that the team figures out. But to me, that's the team. That's them figuring out... I think one year we had 19 players and so our logo was something like, "Everyone in, all the time." And we get a logo or a theme for that year, each year. But for me the values of the program have to stay the same.

You have touched on it there, and you've mentioned that relationships are very important within your program. Do you do any specific team-building activities to help build this? And if not, how are you maintaining these relationships? What's important?

So I don't have a lot of team-building activities, because I feel like if it's me doing it, it's not really a team-building activity. I tell the team a lot, "You have four years," because I coach them for four years, plus or minus. "It's four years and throughout those four years you have to make the most of your freshman year, your sophomore year, your junior year, and your senior year. This is your only chance to be a junior, or your only chance to be a sophomore. It's your team. You have to figure out what you want to do and what is most important."

We ask them at the beginning of the year, "Do you want to win? Or do you just want to make sure everybody plays?" There's two totally different thoughts, and I'm okay with either one. Not really, because I'm super competitive, but I'm okay, because I'm probably going to be here a couple more years. So what do you want? When it comes back out and they say, "So-and-so's not playing," I'm like, "Yeah, but you told me you wanted to win." So for me, it's them... I forget the question. Remind me of the question?

You're doing great, it's very interesting. It was about any specific team building activities, or how you're maintaining relationships.

So the team-building activities, I feel like, is...

I'm pretty strict. I'm pretty hard in pre-season. So for me, going through a drill, going through run-throughs, going through some stuff in practice, demanding a lot out of them is team-building. And we do drills that if you don't go for a ball, and I see it, all of you run. If you don't go for a ball and I miss it, and someone else kicks you out, then nobody runs. So they're pretty good. I've got some great leadership that we've been able to develop over time. Making sure some of those values that we hold dear to the team like, "You go for the ball in every drill you do. There's never a stop." have come from the leadership. The first years come in and the first drill they're like, "Oh, I didn't go for that," and someone just goes, "Get out of the drill." And they're like, "What?" And they're like, "Yeah, that's how you learn to go for the ball."

So I don't really do a lot of team-building stuff, but we do do some talking about it, and I think that that's one of the best things, is we talk about... Julie Foudy has a book that I can't think of the name of it right now [*Choose to Matter*], but we talk a lot about different aspects of that book through the pre-season. It takes five minutes at the end of practice and we talk about one aspect. We do it every year, and every year the players say they learn something new out of it. So I think that's really good in the team-building stuff. But I leave a lot of that up to the team. It's college, so it's a little different. You may not live together at Yale, but you're still eating a lot together, you're still going to school, you're around each other a lot, so I feel like there's a lot of building that goes on.

How do you select team captains? Do you have team captains? And then what are their responsibilities?

At Yale we've been around for over 300 years, so there's some traditions that are in place, and one of them is captains. You only have one captain, and I don't have a vote on it. The team votes the captain, so it's not in my control of what happens. But we have a leadership... We talk to the seniors throughout the Spring. We do some leadership activities. I definitely make leadership everybody's job. The captain obviously has some responsibilities, and there's different things for them, but the captain isn't always my floor captain. I'm always working the sophomores and the juniors to take on some leadership roles as well, as I see those in those people. Yale is a pretty remarkable school. There's a lot of leaders there. Most of the time I have to find some people that are willing to follow, but that's okay.

So you then have a sort of leadership group, kind of thing.

Yes.

Do you meet with them? Do they communicate with you differently than everybody else? How does that work?

I usually meet with the captain once a week during season. Like I said, I don't really pick them, so there's been years where I've had better communicators than not, and then I'll ask some other leaders on the team different questions, just in practice. I'll pull them aside and say, "Hey, how are the first years? Are they doing okay? How are things happening? We want to look at this. What do you think of this?" I talk to my setters... Sometimes my setters aren't captains. I'll talk to them separately. So I think you pick and choose what's important for different people to do. You give responsibilities to those who you want to lead, but maybe don't have opportunities to lead – some non-starters, you make sure that they also have responsibilities.

We talk about roles a lot on the team. Everybody comes in wanting to start, and I have 18 players and six play at once, so more than half of the team is not playing. How do you relate to that? What is your role? Because it's going to take all 18 of us in order to get a championship. You might not be a starter. You might be someone who doesn't even play a lot, or at all. What is your role? Find something of value to cling onto. And I think that that's really important. So we spend a lot of time on that, early on in the season.

You're front-loading a lot of your communication, which I think is very important in creating the relationships. But it sounds like you put a lot of value on everyone contributing to the relationships between everybody.

Yes, definitely. And there's times I have my assistant coaches reach out to certain individuals and say, "Hey, you need to push this person a little harder. You need to make sure you compliment this person more," as I see people struggling or non-struggling in those things. I have a rule that when I stop talking to you is when you have a problem. If I'm talking to you, that means I'm coaching you, that means I have a belief you can be better. So make sure I'm talking to you. So if I'm yelling... Not yelling, but if I'm on you, that's a good thing.

You're at a school that has quite a high value on academics as well as now a great volleyball culture. Are there some causes of conflict from that in the program? And if there are, how do you manage it?

Yeah. I'm pretty strict with them. I don't let them... If they come to me and say, "Hey, I've got a major test that I need to get out of practice early," of course I'm going to let them do that. Academics truly comes first at Yale. It really does. But at the same time, these are young women learning how to manage their time, and they're going to have children, they're going to have families, they're going to have jobs, they're going to have parents, there's going to be a lot of demands on them as women, and they have to be able to handle it. So I'll usually let them leave, but then I'll ask them why? Did you not study on Sunday? What was the Saturday night like? Did you not prepare for this as well as you should have? So maybe this won't happen again.

But the academics come first, and it's something that if I was to go somewhere else it might not be the same. At Yale that's the case, and my job has to happen that way. Our goals are to win an Ivy championship, so everyone in the Ivy League has this hard academic situation. But they also would not have been admitted if they weren't ready to handle it. Yale does a great job through admissions of really being able to make sure people already have those time management skills in place. And yeah, they're young, they're learning, and you have to learn through your mistakes, and you have to make bad decisions in order to improve. So sometimes they're not going to study as much as they should. Then we have conversations about that. Those kind of things. So it's really just an act of balancing.

Academically, my team does better in the Fall, when we're constant than in the Spring when we have more downtime. I know they can handle the academic pressure. And we have all the majors - pre-med, engineering, everything. I don't want them to come in here and then not be able to major in what they want to do. I want to support them and encourage them. I've had players who say, "Hey, I have to take this class and it's in the middle of our practice time. What should I do?" I tell them take the class. Stay after, come in early, do what you need to do to get your extra reps. It's harder when it's a setter, but any other position can kind of do some individual training and be fine. For me, it's the whole package here at Yale. You have to be able to be able to do both.

You have extremely smart young women in your team, obviously. Do you find that contributes to the volleyball IQ at all? Is there any relation there?

I recruit a lot of volleyball IQ. To me that's really important. In the Ivy League, you don't have as many hours to train your athletes as other Division I schools, so you can recruit that great athlete and train them, but I don't have that training time. So I'd rather recruit that really smart player and be able to have her play right away. I think sometimes I have to tell them to just stop thinking and just play. Let your athleticism go. Because we do have some incredible athletes on the team, and sometimes it's just, don't overlook it, don't overanalyze it, just do it. Yeah, my team is way smarter than me. I say things off all the time, and they'll just giggle and know that I'm just wholly wrong in what I'm saying, but it's okay. And they get that I just really want the best for them, so even if I don't say it correctly, they understand.

How big is the roster?

I've had anywhere between 10 players one year, which was really small, to 19. So anywhere in there. I think 16 is probably about ideal. Right now we have a little bit of a larger team, but my numbers will start to go down as well. We have a big class graduating, so it'll eventually get lower.

As coaches we need to be quite knowledgeable in a lot of areas, whether it be technical, tactical, personal. What do you think are the most important qualities for coaching?

Well, we talked about the relationships, I think that's the most. Personnel is extremely important to me. Finding the right mix. It's not about finding the best player. It's about finding the right mix. I talk to my team all the time that the six people that are the best, with the best chemistry, will play. So chemistry to me is really, really important. And I think that's really good. Then I think tactical for me is a little bit more... Which is great, because my assistant's all technical, and I'm all tactical, so it works. Tactical for me, because again, we don't have a ton of training time. If somebody comes in and they're goofy footed, I recruited them being goofy footed, I'm not going to spend time changing them. That's it. If you have a funky arm swing, and you're good enough, as long as it's not hurting your shoulder, we're going to leave it. We're just going to try to make you better at what you do.

And so tactical becomes that thing that's the biggest step between high school and college. It's not that you can blast it cross court. It's, "Hey, we need you to hit at the setter, because their middle is way better than our middle, and we can't have that middle hitting the ball. So if we hit at the setter, the middle can't get the ball." So there are certain things more tactical in that range that we really do, and we try to really emphasize through scouting, through our practices, just making them smarter, better volleyball players. Not necessarily, "Hey, I can crank it here." That's not what we need right now. What we need is this, "I don't need you challenging the libero, I need you scoring."

I'd like to talk about coaching in the preparation – which is anything other than a match – versus the match coaching. You answered it a little bit now, but what do you find to be more important? Does something have more importance, and why?

So it kind of goes back to the pre-season. We lay a lot of the foundation down there, of what's expected, how we're going to get there, what we're going to do to get there, then what we need to do once we're there. I feel like match coaching, to me, is much more about tactics, and about changing maybe what we're doing on the fly, but we should be prepared for every match before we get there. We should know what's happening on the other side. We should know who our personnel is. We should know all of that. I think that it's just important to make sure you're on the same page, that you're not over-promising things to people, and that you're just being an even keel in that regard.

But preparation to me... For me, I want to be the best passing team in the conference, so we spend a lot of time on passing. I recruit people who can pass. We spend a lot of time on defense - I want to be the best defensive team - and serving. So for me, I probably have more of a defensive mindset than an offensive mindset. Some of that is starting to change in the rally score era. You have to be able to side out, but to me, if you can pass and you have a smart enough setter, you should be able to side out. So for me, it's about some basics. Then maybe blocking is in there as well as something that we spend a lot of time on. Offense is probably the thing we spend the least on. But I also feel that most of my players coming in, their shoulders are over-worked, and they already have some tears or something like that, so we don't spend a lot of time hitting. We do spend a lot of time playing against each other, so we do train offense through just playing. But we do a lot more drills of passing and defense and those kind of things.

Can you just expand a little bit more on why these three things are your focus?

I think if you can pass, you can do anything. If you can get the ball up there, you can do a lot with it. We've always been... I don't know why, to be honest. Just my style. I don't like playing someone who can do one thing. I like people who can do multiple things. In recruiting that's what I look at. Instead of just that big thug on the outside that can put the ball away, which might be really important, but it's just probably not as much my style, in that sense. And then serving, I think you can generate a lot of points or get people out of system, and you can do a lot - especially because we know we can side out because we can pass. We can take more risks from the service line, so we can be more aggressive.

Then defense, I've just always been a defensive person. That's probably why.

You talked about the preparation, putting a lot of things in place in the pre-season, which I guess we could define as team concepts. Is there a lot of discussion going into this? I guess each year you have quite a similar culture, and the concepts are the same thing. People know they're coming to Yale, and this is what we're focusing on, this is what we're doing.

Yeah, I would say pretty much. A lot of times, we do activities, and I let them put most of the input in, but I pretty much know what's going to be coming out. I just had individual meetings, and I wanted to ask each player, "What do you want out of next season?" And 90% of them was like, "I want to help the team any way I can." And I was like, "Okay, no, I don't want that answer, I want to know what you want, what your role is." But I just have a lot of really great people in my program, that really want to help the program continue to be successful. So I am almost having to be like, "Be more selfish, than that." No, not really, but that's where the program is right now. I just have a lot of people that want to... "Hey, if I can't start, then I want to be helping from the side lines, I want to do what I can do, anything I can do."

I think I can probably guess from your answers so far, but what are your favorite parts of coaching?

No, you'd be surprised. My absolute favorite time is pre-season, is before the team gets here. I'm a puzzle person. I like to be efficient, so I like to figure out things. For me, the puzzle of how is this team going to develop is really exciting for me. Seeing the new people come in, seeing if the players are in great shape, or maybe they're in good shape but not volleyball shape, or maybe they're in good volleyball shape. Figuring out what the line-ups are going to be, and how good can we be? For me, the pre-season, before we even play matches, before there's a starting line-up, that's one of my favorite times.

And then obviously playing at home, and winning great matches, is a great feeling. And I like recruiting. I enjoy going out and trying to convince people that Yale's the best option for them, which is a pretty good option.

I think there's a lot of different aspects to my job, and I know later on you're going to ask me about staying motivated. To answer that now, to be honest, I'm competitive. I'm a competitive person. So when I go out recruiting, I want to be the best recruiting class in the conference. I want to get that great player. I want to come up with those really good line-ups. So staying motivated... Because every team is different, and I think that's the neat thing about college athletics. It's not just four teams, it's like seven, because when you put in the off-season, you lose those seniors, so other leaders develop, and people come up with different things. Then you gain incoming freshmen and the team dynamics changes. I just think it's an ever-revolving situation, and I really like it. So I have fun, I get so excited about pre-season.

And then obviously during season, for me it's not about winning the big matches. It's about winning all the matches you should, and then doing your best in those other matches. Because I think sometimes you can get caught up in the big matches, and you stumble against those teams that you shouldn't stumble against.

You're right, I didn't guess that.

You've mentioned recruiting a few times as something that you really enjoy, and that's obviously extremely important to what you've built. What are some limitations on recruiting, given that you're an Ivy League school?

The biggest one probably is that we don't have scholarships. Most other Division I schools have 12 full scholarships, and the Ivy League doesn't have any, so the scholarship factor's a little bit different. But typically because the Ivy League students really want to come to the Ivy League, they really reach out to you and they're on top of it, so that is good. The academics narrows my list in recruiting, which some people think that's harder, but it actually makes it easier for me. Yes, I can't go recruit that great stud over there, but I have a smaller list I can work with, which I think is definitely a benefit. So I don't know. I like kind of fiddling with what piece is going to happen, who's going to be the best person for this role looking three years in advance. That's the scary part, with recruiting. It's not just about next year. It happens so early now. Even with some NCAA recruiting rules, it's still you're evaluating younger kids, so you're constantly thinking, who are you going to get?

I tell my team, once you commit to me my job is to go find someone who can beat you out. That's my job. It's your job not to let that happen. But my job is to find better, quicker, more athletic, smarter IQ kids than you. Sometimes that happens, sometimes it doesn't happen, but that's the reality, so I'm not going to recruit someone just because I really like you and I want you to start for four years. I'm going to recruit someone to play, to beat you out. That's my job.

I like talking to parents. I also really believe in Yale. I feel like, even if you take volleyball out of the Yale picture, Yale's an incredible place. I'm selling the Mercedes-Benz of colleges, so that's the nice thing about it.

Just out of curiosity, do any of your players have ambitions of playing volleyball beyond college?

Yes. Yes, actually we have had a couple players go abroad, and play professionally. We've had one so far, but I assume more will, go and play a fifth year of sand [NCAA beach volleyball]. We have had some that have played in years after. But not a ton, because it is Yale, and they're going to med school, or Wall Street, or law school. They're doing stuff.

I don't know if it's as much of a phenomenon in the U.S., but certainly in Europe coaches can be sucked into bigger and better always, and it's hard to find a place to settle down. How did you know that this was the place for you, and when?

I think a couple things go into that. I was at Penn State for ten years, and they were top five school in the country my whole ten years there. So I know what it's like to be at that level, and that's a different level than Yale, and that's okay. Their goals are to win a national championship. Our goal is to win an Ivy championship, so there's a little bit of a difference there. But I had that life, and I did that life, and I know how chaotic that is. In the Ivy League there's certain rules and regulations that we have to take time off. We have to have some downtime. The players don't practice as much. When I got here to Yale, my son was two and my daughter was four months, so I had a very young family. Having some ability to have a great profession as well as be a good mom was really important to me.

And throughout the years there's obviously been job offers and there's been things that I've gone and interviewed for, but I agree that it's not always brighter and greener anywhere else. Through my profession I've worked at places I truly believed in. I think if you're going to recruit you have to believe in what you're selling, and I truly believe in Yale. So to me, I wouldn't take a job just to get to the next level if I didn't believe that that was a great school, that I could really look parents in the eye and say, "This is a great thing for your daughter." I can do that now. I think that's a really neat thing, and I like it. Now my children are much older – both of them will be in college soon – so I could probably go somewhere else, but I really enjoy what I'm doing.

And for a long time, my husband also worked at Yale, so there was both of us here, both of us coaching. Having two people that coach is difficult to begin with, schedule-wise, but we made it work. We got through the tough years when the kids were young with some help from some in-laws and our parents and stuff like that. But now it's just... I love being here.

Looking back, what are some mistakes you've made and things you've learned, or changes you've made from those mistakes?

Sure. I think early on I probably over-trained. But in some ways, I think that was... Like I said, the previous coach had been fired, and it was the team kind of got her fired. I was like, "Hey, be careful what you wish for, here you go, let's run some stairs." So I probably over-trained. Obviously, you always make recruiting mistakes throughout your time, and you have to just be comfortable with those. That's either missing out on someone or recruiting someone who's just not good enough.

Honestly, I look back at games and I think early on in my career, I didn't sub at all. I would really stick with my starters, even though they were struggling. Now I sub a little bit more, which probably that's going to be a mistake in ten years. So I don't think there's a right or wrong answer, but it is a trick to know when do you pull a starter out? Because I don't want people to be worried about making mistakes. I want them to have confidence to go for it. But you have people on the bench that are really good.

I think early in my career I had players that were here [higher level], and players that were here [lower level], so it was pretty easy not to have subs. Now I've got players that are all here [same level]. It's really hard to say to that one person who's just right behind them, "Not going to play you right now." So I tend to sub a little bit more, to give people more opportunities.

I don't know if that's necessarily a mistake. You have to look at your team and evaluate, where is that next person, and how far would that starter go before you pull them? I had a starter once who had seven hitting errors in one set, and my assistants were like, "Are you going to get her out?" And I was like, "No, she's got to get one in eventually." And then she had eight, and then I pulled her. But I think game management is probably where you make sometimes the most noticeable errors, because it's more public, and there's more on the line.

Early on I had a setter who was a senior. We were playing at a site and I had a freshman setter, and we won the first two, we were away, and I thought, "Oh, this would be a great opportunity to get my freshman some playing time." Well, then we ended up losing the next one and a half, and then I put my starting setter back in, and was like, "Win this match for me, please." And we did, but when do you start to try to play people, I think is always different. Now I rarely sub on the road. Unless someone needs to be pulled out, but I never really sub just to let someone get playing time on the road. Maybe at home a little bit more, but my team knows that, so they know going in that it's not an even playing field. People are going to play a lot more than others, and the way I look at it is, you have practice four days a week to impress me, and only two times [matches] on the weekend. So the practice is the most important thing in order to get playing time, not matches.

But yeah, I think there's definitely been some errors along the way, for sure. Those are the ones I think really stick out for me.

Just to jump back on the over-training one, how did you recognize that that was a mistake?

I think it's a mistake because I think we did more sprints and more conditioning in practice, and looking back I'm like, "Oh, we probably should have been passing, or playing defense. I should have done more skill related stuff." And I think some of the drills that I do now, you have conditioning inside of the drill, so you're still touching the ball, but you're still getting some sort of conditioning in. I think it was just so early in my career, I just really wanted to be a hard-ass, in a sense.

And even younger, when I was an assistant, I can remember we lost a huge match, and I wanted to just yell at the team. And the head coach came in and just said, "All right, we got 10 minutes to get on the bus," and I was like, "What? That's it? I don't understand." So I asked Coach Rose why... I was ready to really shake some people, and he's like, "They don't listen to you after a loss. Nobody's thinking clearly. On Monday, we'll talk about it, and they'll listen, because everybody will have gotten over their heartache by then. But on a really bad loss, it's easier just to say, '10 minutes, let's get on the bus, let's go,' We'll talk about it another day, or not."

I've had matches where we've lost a really important game on a Friday night, and we have to play Saturday, and I'll say to the team, "We're going to go back to the hotel, we're going to shower, and within this time frame you can grieve. But when you come to meet with me again, we are focusing on the future." And I think that's a really important... To be able to turn it like that I think is a really important thing. It's something I think athletics teaches people so much.

I know I keep rambling, but I had a player who.... She was in astrophysics, so she was extremely bright. She said in a thing for engineering, "Being an athlete taught me how to overcome losses, how to overcome things." And when she was a senior, a lot of her friends maybe didn't get into their top med school or get into their top job or whatever, and they were so devastated. [She said] "I was like, 'All right, next one,' because I was so used to being able to bounce back after having that heartache, and being an athlete really teaches you that."

So I think coaches that dwell too much on the loss, or yell and scream at their players after losses... I know I'm not listening to anybody after a loss. Everybody feels like, "It's my fault!" So nobody's really listening, so there's nothing constructive happening until you take some time to get over it. Then you go forward. I think that that's something that I learned early on that was probably something I wouldn't have done had I not been with Coach Rose for as long and seen it happen and see how it works better.

On that, do you have a set routine that you... You don't speak to the players after a loss, I guess, but...

No, I mean we do. I think all losses are different. There's losses where you literally are just not as good as the other team. There's losses where you messed up. So I think there's different ways to handle it. But typically, when we have a heartbreaking loss, a lot of times I'm very quick with my... It's more logistics. "Okay, let's meet back here in two hours to go over tomorrow's scouting report." Or if it's a Saturday and we don't have anything, I'll talk about Monday's practice. I'll just give them some logistical things to think about, and then we'll talk again as a group at another date, when I've cooled off too.

Sometimes I'm really mad and I'm going to say something I'm going to regret, and I don't want to be that person. So a lot of times it's also just so I can cool down, and then look and say, "Okay, what really did happen in this match? Did I not make a good enough change during the match, or did we just have a lousy week in practice and so it resulted in this match?"

How are you guys integrating statistics and technology into your program? Could you give us some examples?

Yeah. Probably not as good as we should, because there's so much stats out there, but I'm also kind of a gut coach in that sense. My second assistant is very good with stats. He comes from the men's game, which I think has more statistical analysis, and deals more with it. Like I said, I feel like for me the six best players are going to start with the best chemistry, so it's not just the best hitter in our gym. If nobody can stand her and our setter will never set her, then she's not really helping us. So it's looking at some stats... We do a lot of passing stats. We do a lot of things figuring out if we're going to pass with two, we're going to pass with three, who should be the libero, things of that nature.

During a match, I look at... I used to keep stats, me personally, in a match. Just a zero, plus, minus kind of stat and I could say that So-and-so's having three or four errors in a row, because sometimes in a match you miss those things. You just have to figure out what stats are important to you, and then really be able to trust that. Knowing what rotations are important to start in, what rotations the other people that you're playing against...

I'm, like I said, probably much more of a defensive coach, so I work a lot on what the opponent... How do we stop this? And how do we do this? I am starting to try to think more of, they've got to stop us too. So I think that's something that's a new challenge in my life, is thinking more offensive.

But for me, it's much more, how do I stop this? Or how do we affect this? And stats will help show you that. But I don't know specifically if I can really tell you which ones I always look at. I have my assistant go through it, he goes through all the numbers and then tells me what is relevant. And then I'm like, "Okay, we'll do that."

Why did you want to be a part of a series of female coaches?

I think it's terrific. I know I'm going to probably talk about some of the other things that you're going to ask me about, but there's not a lot of role models. In the United States, Pat Summitt at Tennesee was one of the most successful women's basketball coaches ever, and she happened to be a woman. But I also feel that men have most of the jobs at the top of the volleyball realm right now. Most of the top, I would say 10, maybe 20, 90% of it's men. And there's definitely been some ways that can change there. There's definitely some up-and-coming female coaches. There's a lot more younger coaches than there are older coaches. So part of me wanted to be a part of this, because I think it's important to grow. I think women make great coaches because we care about the relationship side of it more. And I think the hard part is the balancing of your life.

What are some of the barriers that we face?

I think the family. I think women, to be honest, aren't as aggressive asking for raises, asking for things. We're just happy that we're where we're at, instead of saying, "I've done this, I deserve this." I think that's something that maybe 20 or 30 years from now will be more neutralized. I look at it like, my mother didn't have an opportunity to play college sports, and then Title IX came and I had an opportunity. And then I stayed with it, and I look at my daughter, and she will have better opportunities than I did. And I think it's going to just take some time.

But I think the family is a big one. Like I said, I left Penn State to be an at-home mom, because I didn't think I could do both and be successful. I was halfway here and halfway here, and I was never really good at both. But I think being a head coach helps, because you can do your own schedule, you can determine what tournaments and when to go. You can do those things. But you have to take some lumps along the way, same as men, not controlling your schedule.

And I think sometimes financial. Sometimes it's just also the financial burden of... Are you the breadwinner? If you're married, will someone follow you along as you make these steps? Those kind of things.

So there's definitely some barriers between the two, but I definitely see it changing. There's a lot of really good... I would say over the last five years, in women's volleyball, the top 20 are probably mostly men, but the 20 through 50 are probably a lot of females. So they're gaining some traction.

Just two things from that. One, the family support. It's definitely something I've heard of many times, that it's difficult having a family and being a coach. Are there things that can change that can make it better, that there can be more support for women to be in this role?

Yeah, I think the NCAA can do some things. I think they can limit the number of recruiting days. I think that's where the hard part comes. I think NCAA made some rules that actually disadvantage women, or young mothers. They shortened when we can recruit, which means now we have to recruit every weekend, where before you had a longer... Five months to recruit, and you weren't out every weekend. So you could balance it between your staff. Now I think it's 80 days you can go out recruiting. It should be lowered. I think the NCAA, if they lower that and they widen when you can go, then hey, if I have to be gone for twice a month on a weekend as a young mother, okay. But if I'm gone every weekend as a young mother, it really is tough to be able to say goodbye... You're leaving Thursdays, coming back late Sunday, and then you're back at work on Monday and you're not getting any break. So I think there's some things of that.

Right now, May has always been kind of a quiet period, so I always was the best mom in May. That was the month I went into the classrooms all the time when they were young, and would volunteer, and I would be able to come home early and be home when they were home. May was my month. May was my mother day month. So we had to pick and choose. And the right job. Yale was a perfect job for me at a perfect time. But finding those things, and finding maybe bosses that also understand that I can't be out all the time, even though I want to, and even though I care enough about the program, I also want to be a good role model to my children, and saying you can do both I think is important.

I think that's the kid issue.

The other thing that I wanted to ask about was, you mentioned that as females we're generally not as aggressive asking for things, whether it be a raise or a better job or anything like that. Is that something that you touch on with your players, given that they're young women as well?

Yes, I do. We talk a lot about making sure that they understand their worth, and their value, and that they're going to run into obstacles along the way, just like I will. I do let them leave practice early to study, but I don't want it. This is just one aspect that you have to learn that's not going to be given to you later in life, and you've got to be able to manage that. So we do, we talk a lot about it, fighting the uphill battle. To me that's part of a being a coach, especially with these extraordinary women, making sure that they become extraordinary leaders in their time.

So what has been important for you as a woman to continue on your coaching journey? Like mentor, support system...

I have a great husband. I've got understanding kids. When they were young, sometimes it was hard when my daughter would be like, "Oh, well So-and-so's mother brings her backpack here, or does this, or carpools us," and I was like, "Yeah, you're learning independence. That's what you're learning right now." So I see her now as a young woman, and I know I've done a good job with making sure she's able to handle herself in the world. But I think you have to have a good support system. Both my husband and I are only children. We don't have brothers or sisters or aunts or uncles or cousins or anything, so we really relied on our family a lot to help – our parents and my in-laws, to come and help with the kids.

And we had a nanny for many years that was great, and could watch them, and I think that was one of the best things we ever did, instead of putting them in daycare. Just having someone who came to the house. She was here 'til my youngest was I think starting kindergarten, so it was really nice to have some support in that realm. But you have to find out what you can, and it takes a village. You have to rely on... Again, I would ask people, "Hey, I can't carpool in March and April, but come May, I can do both ways all the time." So you had to make friends in the community, and make sure that your daughter could go to soccer practice, or your son to wherever he was going, and those kind of things, and make sure it was covered.

There might be some crossover from previous questions here, but what are some of the challenges that you face that are unique to female coaches, if any?

I think the fact that there isn't a lot of female coaches is one challenge. I think sometimes you get overlooked. People early on in my career probably didn't really expect us to have as much success as we have. Those kind of things. And I think there's some disadvantages, but I wouldn't want to be a man, I'm happy to be a woman. I think there's huge advantages to being a woman. And I think that's something you just have to find. What can you go out and grab? What can you go out and get? And again, pick and choose your battles, pick and choose the top five. If I had a [prospective recruit's] coach that thought maybe I wasn't as good as the guy, maybe

I just didn't deal with that coach. And then their kids didn't get to Yale. That's kind of a problem – for them, not for me. So I think you just have to pick and choose when we want to play that role, and when not to. But I think women are great at what we do, and being able to control the obstacles that are in front of us.

If there was one misunderstanding or stereotype of women coaches that you would want to clear up or argue against, what would it be?

I don't think so. I haven't really noticed it for me any stereotype. Maybe softer, but I'm not really that much softer than anybody. I don't think there's really... I haven't really found that. I can't really answer that.

Last couple questions. Do you have any books that you would recommend that have been influential?

So we use this book, Jeff Janssen, *The Team Captain's Leadership Manual*. It's an 11 chapter, easy guide to leadership. We use this with all my senior classes. We go through the book. They interview different people, short small little assignments that they can do during class time. I love that one. I mentioned the Julie Foudy book earlier. But other than that, I'm not really a big book reader.

And to finish up, do you have any advice for coaches just starting out in their career?

Yeah. Don't get overwhelmed. Prioritize, prioritize, prioritize. Find out what you're good at, and do that. Find people that can help you in the things that you're not good at. Don't try to be great at everything. Just try to find... Be really good at one or two things, and be a specialist, and then you can grab more once you become a specialist in those skills, whatever they are. Whether you're really good at logistics, whether you're really good with people, whether you're really good at training. But you don't have to be great at everything. There's space and time that needs each of those skills, and to be able to do really great in one of those skills I think is important.

Chapter Three

Audrey Cooper

Scottish coach Audrey Cooper led the Great Britain women's team in the 2012 Olympics in London, and helped them achieve their goal of a historic win at the Games. She is an Olympian in her own right, as well, having represented Team GB in the inaugural Beach competition in Atlanta in 1996. After her Olympic coaching experience, Audrey coached in Switzerland, joined the FIVB Coaching Commission, then became the Technical & Talent Director for Volleyball England. After then spending time working on coaching education programs at UK Sport, she moved on to the Football Association where she heads up women's coach development. She remains active at the club level of volleyball in England, however. All this experience gives Audrey a unique perspective and she's able to really articulate a lot of parts of coaching – why and how we do things – and offers a lot of great examples from her career.

***

Could you start by telling us about your history and experience in volleyball? How did you get to where you are now?

I guess I started playing volleyball in secondary school. I was 12 and volleyball was certainly not on my radar. It wasn't a sport I was familiar with. As a young girl, I played football [soccer] in the streets. Then I went to secondary school and took up [field] hockey, and then all of a sudden fell in love with volleyball pretty soon after that. I was really lucky that my school teacher just happened to be the Scotland national team coach for women. He got volleyball going in the school, and from there, as I said, I fell in love with it. I represented the school, the county and the national team. Then, at a very young age of 18, I took the journey from Scotland to London. I told my mom it was for my career, but it was really for volleyball because volleyball in England was a higher level and they played in Europe and so forth.

I ventured to London and spent 25 years there playing for a number of clubs. We played in Europe, getting to round three of European competitions. I then went on from indoor volleyball to play beach volleyball - initially for some fun, but that then became really quite serious. It was a demonstration sport in '92, and so there was an opportunity to qualify for Olympics in '96.

Myself and an English player got together and started playing on the world tour, and we qualified for the Olympics in '96. We were the only British team ever to qualify for an Olympics, so we were pretty proud of that. Then I kind of went back into indoor, got involved in coaching my club, and then the England national team. From there, I went on to coach the GB team going into the London 2012 Olympics. I spent five years with the GB team, then a year after the Olympics, coaching professionally at NUC [women's pro team Switzerland].

Then I came back to England and stayed in volleyball. I became the Technical Director of the national governing body. Then things changed a little bit here in England in terms of funding, and I suddenly found myself in coach development in football. That takes me way back to when I was a young girl back into football, but clearly my passion is volleyball.

You were a pretty high level player - an Olympian. How do you think that's influenced your coaching, or what are some character traits that have carried over that have helped you?

I think we often talk about what are your values? What are your DNA? Part of my DNA is about hardworking commitment. The Americans used to remind us that we were a tiny little island - that you had to be resilient. We have to be resourceful because the sun doesn't always shine in England.

In my time as a beach athlete - an Olympian - we had to just find ways to train, find ways to improve, to go up the levels and the ranking. That stood me in really good stead to be really resilient and resourceful, which kind of took me into my coaching career with GB. There was some really big ... We call it a rocky road. There was definitely a rocky road with the journey I went on in coaching and to be able to overcome hurdles.

I'm a little bit like if you say I can't do it, I'm probably going to go and do it. If we say that it's not going to be possible, then I'll find a way to make it possible. I think that as an athlete put me in good stead to be a coach. I never really thought I'd experience some of the hurdles I did in coaching. But certainly that's put me in good stead to move into coaching.

It's just not that often we find the really high level players as high level coaches as well. I'm always curious to ask a bit more about that question.

I think you only reflect on it afterwards in terms of when you were an athlete, the sort of things that really helped to develop you. Even just communication. We're a team sport, so how to communicate, how to work with people that are different to you. Because I'm sure you've had teammates where you think, "She is a pain in the butt." Find a way to work with them, and there'll be those you work with really, really well. That's the same in coaching. But you've got to find a way to work and communicate and get on and get the best out of people. That's what I tried to do.

When I played indoor volleyball, I was a setter. As a setter, you're running the show. I was a captain, so you're trying to get the best out of folks. Those attributes that I developed as a player really, really helped me when I moved into coaching.

Being a setter as well - a tactician, if you like - you're really trying to expose your position and get the best out of your teammates. That again really helped transition into coaching. I had that mindset, because I never really knew whether coaching was going to be for me. But bizarrely, people would say, "Yeah, I think you'll make a good coach." I was like, "Well, who knows?" Because when you're playing, you just want to play. But certainly a lot of what I experienced as an athlete, and what I learned as an athlete, definitely set me up for my coaching journey.

Would you be able to talk about some of your coaching influences?

Certainly the coach who got me involved in volleyball, he was just an incredible individual. His name was Bob Stokes and he set up volleyball in our school. He was already the national team coach. He took himself off to places like Japan to learn what volleyball's like in another continent and brought that back to us in a small country of Scotland. He'd bring sort of new ways of doing things. He was definitely an influence.

I had another coach called Jefferson Williams [featured in the first Wizards book] who had come from Canada. He arrived in England and he brought an approach to coaching in a different kind of thinking and was very technically minded. That influenced me. I took a lot from Jeff from a kind of technical perspective.

Another chap was a guy called Ian Goswell. He was a coach, but he was more like a mentor to me. He had incredible people skills, incredible. I learned a lot from him about how to get the best out of people and also recognizing more about myself, develop my own self-awareness.

Those are my influences in and around England. Then internationally, it would be a female coach. Lang Ping has been just such a massive influence. I had an opportunity back in, I think it was 2008 or 2009 where I was on an elite coach program in the UK for coaches from different sports. We had the chance to go and meet someone and go and work with someone. I got the chance to go over to Colorado and watch the USA team train and how they operated, how she used staff, how she got the best out of players, what their training program was like, how they used analysis during training. Her being a female was a really big influence on me, and continues to be a big influence. I'm always watching out for where she is and what she's doing because there aren't that many females at top level. She's certainly been an influence.

I've had an opportunity to work a little bit with the likes of Hugh Mc-Cutcheon. I sit on the FIVB Coaching commission, and I obviously came across Hugh at the Olympics. I think he's a very humble individual. Really, really humble and knowledgeable individual. He's certainly influenced my career and I still watch out for what he's doing now in Minnesota. He's been an international coach and he's gone into university.

And there have been many other people who've played a part in my coaching career.

Those are some nice names. Your coaching philosophy, how's that changed over time?

Well, there's a story here.

I remember I went on this course called Elite Coach. It was a UK Sport course. I was on this three year journey with coaches from other sports. It was all in the buildup to the Olympics to support coaches to be as best as they could. The very first workshop - of which there were about 12 - you had to take your coaching philosophy to the workshop, and I thought, "Oh my goodness, I've never been asked that before. What's my coaching philosophy?"

First of all, I looked it up in the dictionary and it talked about it being your guiding principles. I was thinking a little bit more about that. I presented what was my coaching philosophy. Quite a bit clearly linked to my values. Over that three year time it evolved - and it continues to evolve - But it started off with "Perseverance and belief equals performance". From there it evolved into "People, perseverance and belief in people equals performance". Then I added another P to it (It was kind of P exercise). Planning came into it. "Persevere and planning and belief in people equals performance."

Those are, I guess, the bits that still hold true to me today. Having been a bit of a planner, a little bit anal, perseverance that I talked about before is me through and through. Then belief in people, because often people don't have self-belief. I think it's really important as a coach to believe that somebody might not be an international superstar, but they can be better, and getting them to see that. If you bring all of that together, they can get a performance.

It's like you plan for a match. You think about how you're going to deal with the offsets. You've got to persevere. But you've got to sometimes instill belief and build on the belief that players have to get the performance on a weekend or whatever. That's kind of what is my philosophy. I write it out like it's a little algebra test with pluses and equals and so forth in it.

It evolved. It's been a journey of developing my own personal level of self-awareness - to know who I am and what I stand for, what I'm really all about and where that comes from. That's helped me really shape my philosophy. I was like, "What on earth is a philosophy really?" It sounded really posh. But clearly I had it. I just hadn't articulated it.

Did you find articulating it sort of helped you to hold yourself to those standards as well?

Yeah, it did. Throughout my career, the other great skill that you need to have as a coach is the ability to reflect. When I've wavered off that, sometimes it's been too late when I've realized it. But where I've been able to go back and look at that philosophy and think, "Right. What is happening now? Am I staying true to my philosophy?" it certainly helped me. It took me back and grounded me to make me go back to what I truly believed in.

There've been a few times I went off that, which was where it didn't go quite as I'd maybe expected. But that allowed me to come back and ground and reflect and go, "Right. This is what I'm all about. This is what I believe in. This is the direction I think I need to go in." I truly would recommend that to any young coach or experienced coach, to really understand what your philosophy is. Because it drives from just when you walk through the door in the training ground. That should be who you are and what you stand for.

What about training methodology? What are some differences between a training session back then and now? A difference in the methodology.

I guess I don't do as meticulous planning because I'm not a full-time coach. But I guess I feel pretty confident. I have a full-time job now, whereas before coaching was my life, but I pretty much know my plan, what I'm going to do. But it won't be written out in a meticulous detail. It won't be part of a big written season plan, but it will be linked to what we're trying to achieve. We're always having objectives. That's continued. I'll know what it is we want to achieve.

First and foremost, I try and observe the mood in the gym. Because the people I'm coaching now, they do it more for fun. They've got jobs as well, but they're competitors. I've got to think about what the mood is when I walk in. I've got a plan and objective, but I feel the mood.

Actually, as I've got older, I do that much better than I did as a younger coach. Whereas before, I was a young coach, "I've got a plan. This is a session. We're playing so-and-so on the weekend. This is what we're going to do." But you learn over time that you've got to be able to adapt. You've got to flex the plan based on where the players are at, where you're at, what your day has been like, and what else is going on around you and in your environment.

I always remember - this stayed with me from a young age - I worked in business for a long time, Lauren, before I got the real fabulous opportunity to coach full-time. When I was in marketing it was, "Where are we now? Where are we trying to get to? How are we going to get there?" That's something that stayed with me for - I'll show my age now - 25, 30 years. That is almost the backdrop to my sort of methodology and planning. Where are we now? Where are we trying to get to? How are we going to get there? It's so simple and clearly lots of layers to that. That's something that I still kind of have in mind. Whether it's for the session that day or the month or the season, I'll being really clear about that. It sounds a little bit anal, but it's very simple.

You took over Great Britain with five years to go to the Olympics, right?

Yeah.

What were the goals and what did you focus on when you took over the program? It's a big question, but let's try and tackle it.

I guess the backdrop is first that we had players from all over the UK - England, Scotland, Ireland, Wales. The majority of players came from England, with a few really fabulous players from Scotland. But they were all training twice a week, playing on a weekend. A big part of our first year, 18 months, almost two years, was getting our players up to a level where they could physically sustain playing tournament volleyball at the level that we were going to be asked to compete in the Olympics. It was developing physically and technically. That was almost the first part of the five year plan. We used a really simple long-term player development methodology of learning to train, training to train, training to compete, training to win, et cetera. That was the backdrop to our five year plan. But the very early part of it was about developing physically and technically.

Then we pulled together a program, a competitive program, where we had to experience playing against teams from the different continents and what that meant. Then from there, we had to find a way to play. Because it'd be nuts if we tried to play like Russia because we're not 6'6". It'd be crazy if we tried to play like Japan in their quick speed type of pace. We have to come up with something that was a hybrid model that was a way that we could find that we could compete. Because in five years, you don't go from 69th in the world to top five. That's just not really achievable. We had to be realistic. We had a realistic plan knowing that we wanted to compete. We were really sure we wanted to be able to compete. Our goal was to win a game at the Olympics. The stretch goal was two games in the pool. We knew that targeting a team from the African nation, if we drew them in our pool, it would be a goal for us.

We made sure that part of our competitive program was playing against teams from, as I said, the different continents. We knew their style of play and we knew how we could match up to it. That's a very shortened version of kind of what the plan was.

There was a big bump in the road on that journey. As a program, we were funded by UK Sport. With two years out to the games, our funding was cut. That meant no centralized program, no SportsLine services, S&C, physio, we were on our own.

First, what I had to do - and is linked to one of the questions I think you might ask me - is about the GB players and getting them professional contracts. Because we already had a half a dozen or eight people playing in pro clubs during the season, but we had to get the whole squad contracts.

We worked really closely with a few agents to get our players placed in clubs from Slovenia to Switzerland to France to Germany to Italy in the A2 league, et cetera. We did that pretty successfully. The whole team managed to get a contract to play abroad professionally. Then they would come back and be with us with GB.

Meanwhile, I'm busy raising money and finding solutions to how we would be able to compete and so forth, and worked with a whole load of partners. Which is a massive bump in the road, which comes back to the resourcefulness and the resilience piece. Then we go and we compete at the Olympics and we beat Algeria and we get our win at the Olympics. Which was just unbelievable through all the hardships.

It was an amazing journey fraught with lots of bumps in the road, but it ended being a huge success because we were the most successful Great Britain volleyball team at the Olympics between the men and the women and the beach. We were really proud of that, having lost our funding two years out.

I've got a couple of things, but the first one, there's no longer a full-time program, right?

Yeah. We are in rebuild mode. Obviously, at the Olympics, you compete as Great Britain. But prior to that, we competed as home nations. The early part of that five year process is bringing those players together. But now it's evolved. It's gone back. You compete as England, Scotland, Ireland, and Wales. The England piece has taken some time, but we're now in rebuild mode. We're bringing players together from our junior programs, and there's now an England senior team. It seems like that was a long time ago. There were a few things happened between 2012 and now, but there is no longer a full-time program.

But we do have some others here in England where we work with universities. We have what we call the Senior Academy. Our best players get the chance to go and study, get a degree like they do in the States. Some of them gets some scholarship and then they get to do almost daily training. They get an S&C program, et cetera. We suggest to our best athletes to go to our Senior Academy. They will represent England, and some will go and play abroad and hopefully get some professional contracts.

You mentioned you kind of developed a hybrid style of play. I wanted to ask about team concepts, and I think we can sort of jump in there a

little bit. Could you go into a bit more detail about why, and what that entailed?

I guess, we had a real mixture of the type of player that was for GB. We had a few players who, I guess you would call - there's probably an American term - a little bit of a hammer. They were strong. They were powerful. Then we had players who were really quick, and laterally quite quick. We tried to play a little bit of a Japanese style. Knowing that we had a few girls that played really strong, we had to be able to still deliver a quality ball to the area, for example. We had to work really quite a lot with our setters to be able to adapt to a ball that's a little bit slower that allows the girls who had a hammer to be able to have options. Then we worked with the girls that had really good lateral speed to be able to play really quick. We often played with a double quick and with our right side.

Traditionally – certainly in men's volleyball - the right side is the hammer. Whereas where we played it was somebody who was just really quick and played lots of slides and lots of second tempo type balls. We had a real variation.

But one of the backdrops to what we did really well was our defense. What I'd call the big players had to have good, solid defense skills. Because what was going to determine whether we would win sets and win matches was our ability to defend well against some really, really good teams; and clearly having a plan as to how we were going to do that.

That was the kind of hybrid piece around the offense strategy. Then the defense, everybody had to work really hard to be physically good to stay low to the ground and to be able to defend, and defend resiliently, and have bravery about our defense. It might not always look pretty, but there would have to be bravery about picking a ball up and keeping the ball alive.

Sometimes scrappy volleyball can win you volleyball matches. We were fighters and we scrapped a lot in defense. Then trying to have a bit of a variation in our offense and playing to the strengths of the players that we had. Because we definitely did not have 6'6" players in abundance. It was making the best of the profile of the players that we had.

How did that differ to when you took over at NUC for example, and developing the concept of play there?

I guess there were definitely some similarities. We had some really super talent that was both Swiss and a bit of mix of American and some folk from elsewhere. It was similar in the sense that you're trying to get the best out of the player profile that you had. There were many similarities.

We certainly had a few hammers. We had somebody who was incredibly quick off the floor – Lindsey - in terms of being able to play these double quick type of balls. We had a really super setter who was really quite talented who could spray the ball around. I think the bit where we weren't so hot was in our service reception. Technically, we were not the best. Again, we had to graft really hard and we had to make sure we had a setter who was incredibly mobile and could make the best out of nothing.

There were some elements I took from GB into the NUC program. But certainly, they were a little bit different mentally. They were competitive, but their attitude to volleyball was a little bit different to what I'd experienced in the national team - on and off the court - and I wasn't used to that. I was used to, it was all relatively serious and it was all about going to a major competition and being the best you could possibly be. It was quite difficult for me to adapt to that.

Let's move into their culture development a little bit. You've touched on a few things in terms of the style of play, which kind of lends itself to the culture as well. But is there anything else you want to discuss about how you developed the culture at GB, and then maybe at NUC as well, and some other examples?

It was a really important part because, as I said, we had people kind of coming from all areas of the UK - different backgrounds, both personally and from a volleyball perspective, and just really different people. We did quite a lot of work on who we were as a team, what we stood for. We came up with eight, let's call them behaviors, that we agreed and the team came up with that we were really going to live and die by.

But before we did that, we tried to learn about each other. We did some of these, they're kind of like personality trait type tests. This one was called SDI. It's called the Development Inventory. It's about who you are when everything's going well and who you are when things are not going so well. We all tend to change our behaviors. It was understanding each other better and our behaviors, both as a playing group, but also as a staff. So we could work out how we get the best from each other. Because you'd have personalities that were so different that were getting frustrated with each other. We learned about each other and how to get the best out of each other.

We used the phrase, "how to ring each other's bells". The way we do things around here, we had an agreement, this is what we were going to live and die by. We were able to reward, but also able to challenge each other if we went away from those agreed behaviors. That was something we did really, really well in GB. It was the catalyst for bringing the team together to really gel as a unit.

I'm a big believer in that. You've got to get the culture, you've got to get the environment right in order for people to feel that they can really excel. But you got to know each other to know how to get the best out of each other. You've got to know how far you can push someone and when somebody needs an arm round, and when somebody needs just a little gentle nudge or a big push. But we're all different, and recognizing that we're all different.

It was a big learning experience for me as a coach because I thought everybody would just be like me. Then, when I very quickly realized that you can get success in many different ways, the view in our sport being a team sport is how you get them all to work together being so different. That was a huge learning for me because I didn't understand it at first. I'd think, "Why is so-and-so lazy?" But that was lazy through my lens. They weren't lazy. It was probably something behind that, and it was just a different way of approaching it that happened to be different to me. Those were definitely big learnings in my coaching and how to get the right culture and not overdoing your strengths.

Did you do any team-building things to help that culture? Do you have any examples if you did?

Yeah. This initiative that I've just spoken about was when we came together away from the volleyball court or we spent time together. We also did some stuff prior to the Olympics where - wait to hear this - we were living in a fire brigade training center because they offered us free accommodation. We thought, "Brilliant, what a super idea. Let's take the girls into a fire. What a great idea!" We had them all up in breathing operator sets, took them in there to go and save dummy babies. They had to bring a hose reel in, they had to take a BA set apart, et cetera. I took them totally out of their volleyball environment into something where it would gel them as a team.

Then we did the cycle ride. We did what was supposed to be a 250 mile cycle ride from the north of England to Trafalgar Square in London to raise money because we'd lost our funding. It set out as a fundraising exercise, but it was one of the best team-building things we could ever have done. It took us five days to do it. We stayed in army bases. We had sore back sides. We had to push people and help each other up the hill, and the team just kind of came together. It was just a super experience. The learning from that is, get outside of your environment and get to know each other in a different environment because you find out way more about people.

I can't say that I've heard those examples before.

That was one of the things they were quite good at in terms of doing team building and getting to know your teammates.

Changing gears a bit, leadership and captain selection. How have you, in the past, selected team captains, and what have their responsibilities been?

I think that's always an interesting one, to decide what should a captain look like. What kind of leadership qualities? It's quite difficult to find someone who will have all the qualities that you need. But certainly being a role model is one, that they're enacting what it is you say you stand for. That they stand by that and they demonstrate it day in, day out. That kind of quality of leadership and whatever our eight behaviors were, the captain had to display those, but they might not have all of them in abundance.

Having a vice captain, a kind of #2 who had maybe some other qualities that your captain didn't have was something that I think I've done through my whole coaching career. Having somebody who's the captain, for sure, then having somebody who backs them up. So that when they're having a bad day, that somebody else can pick up the reigns and lead the team.

There'll be some captains who are vocal and some who are just really great at doing things quietly and getting on and delivering their job and really living your values. There'll be those that are pretty vocal and are great at motivating. Depending on the attributes of the individual, but certainly someone who can get on with people, but they don't have to be the best friend. That they can check and challenge them are some of the qualities that you would look for.

It's not easy while you're trying to perform your own job to try and help get the best out of your teammates. I've always looked at it in terms of, "What does the team need?" What kind of qualities, and what are our values, and would a captain stand by those values and live them every day? Then always having the number two who can back up a captain because it's a big responsibility being the captain.

Have you always selected the captains yourself? Has there ever been a team vote, or has it always been you choosing?

I've kind of tried a few different ways. I think when I was the England coach for some time, at the very start, I thought, "No. Okay. We use the staff for selecting." Then I thought, "Okay, let's see where the players would go with this."

Of course, you've always got to be mindful the players will pick their friends or who they know best. But depending on the group of players you have, if you know their relatively mature and they know what it is you're going after, then I would ... What I've ended up doing is getting the players view on it, then as the staff deciding who the best person would be. The players will see it through one lens, but as a staff we'll see a little bit wider in terms of what the team needs. I would get the view, but ultimately I would select that as a staff.

As coaches, we need to be pretty knowledgeable in a lot of areas - whether it be technical, tactical, or personal. What do you think the most important qualities are for a coach?

This wouldn't have been what I would have said a few years ago, but what I would say now is the qualities of a coach is how to get the best out of the players. If you have that in your tool belt - that you really understand people and how to get the best out of them - that's just such an amazing quality.

But you can't do that alone. You have to have a good tactical brain and be able to not just come up with a plan, because anybody can come up with a plan. They can do some analysis and come up with a plan. But you've got to then coach it and get the best out of the players in terms of executing the plan. I think I always felt like I wanted to be a master tactician because I really enjoy that part of the game.

Being a setter, you will know that's just such a thrill when you create a one-on-one and you see the players being successful. The tactical side always attracted me, but that alone for me is not the be-all and end-all.

It's about how you get the best out of the team when they're on a high and when they're on the low. Because the plan has to be executed.

If you're a national team coach there's an expectation that players will come with a level of technical ability, but that's not always the case. I think you have to understand the technical side of the game, but it wouldn't be my top priority. You have to obviously develop the technical ability of service reception, or jump float serving, or whatever it might be. You have to have a real understanding of that, but certainly knowing how to get the best out of the players would now be my number one. And being tactically astute to be able to deal with the moments in the game. Because, like you'll know, you have a plan, but shit happens. You've got to be able to deal with the what ifs in a match. That ability to be able to think on the spot and make really, really good decisions.

Between coaching in training and coaching in the match, do you find one to be more important and why?

Yeah. I mean, certainly it's different pressure, isn't it?

We always try as coaches to apply pressure in training that will be like a game. Which is really, really difficult to do. I think the challenge in the game is to be able to think in the moment. But also, if you've done your job really well, the players can do the thinking and make the changes. That's the holy grail of coaching - that you sit on the side, not quite twiddling your thumbs, but the team takes care of themselves. That is the ultimate, the empowering the players to do it. Allowing them to do that in training to empower them. You've got to do that if you want to expect them to do it in a match. But you see so many coaches drill, drill, drill, drill, "I'm the coach. I'm the boss. This is how we're training." Get to a match, and then after the match go, "We lost. Well, the players didn't do what they were supposed to do." Because you didn't allow them to think for themselves.

The question about what was one versus the other, I think my answer is one's got to compliment the other, honestly. That's not a cop-out. One has to, because you can't expect the outcome if you don't do it in training.

When you are coaching in club, is there a difference to the way that you approach the training - the week's training load, amount of sessions, etc. - in different phases of the season, pre-season, finals?

Yeah. I'd say for sure that with the GB program everything was really planned out pretty meticulously. We learned quite a lot about that, because we'd never really been in a full-time program before. But certainly there would be more loading in the beginning of a season and weight, so it'd be heavier. But what we learned over time is that you've got to continue that loading at different points in the season, because otherwise you come to the end of the season, then you've run out of gas. We learned about what that looked like. It was making sure that we were evaluating it in season as well.

Everyone thinks you front load it and you'll last the season and it just doesn't work like that.

I remember that actually from my playing days, Lauren. I traveled for seven years around the world playing on the world tour. We went through a phase where you couldn't access a gym and we were like, "Well, we can't access a gym, so we can't do our loading." It was really a disaster. We had to find new methods to make sure we were still loading whilst we were competing in a tournament and still doing something to make sure there was an element of loading or a different type of training that maintained ...

It's a bit like you just have to keep filling the gas up, because it has to sustain you through a season. Especially if you're going into a national team, you're going into a tournament play. People that play for any professional clubs during the season, you need have recovery time as well. Maybe you play just on a weekend, or you might play one day in the week and one on the weekend. When you play a national team you tend to play a few games over a few days.

You've really got to be thinking about what loading, what strength you need to have to be able to maintain a tournament and not just week in and week out. But rest and recovery is something I'd add to this that you've got to build in time to really recharge both physically and mentally. I think in our first year, we just went really, really hard because we knew we had to develop the players physically. But we learnt very quickly that you need to have rest and recovery and regenerate as well.

Which is really tough for a lot of players that play pro around and then directly to national team. It's not an easy skill.

It's not.

All right. What about your philosophy towards building and selecting your staff? What are you looking for and what roles do your staff do?

I'm giving away all my good and my bad here, but in the initial days I was probably looking more for people who were a bit like me. It's like, "Yeah, okay, let's get behind it. This is the way we're going to drive forward." But as my career went on - and it wasn't always possible by the way - it was good to get people who complemented what you did.

It's a bit like Ian that I mentioned before. I was pretty much driving the technical and the tactical areas. I brought him in because he had just super people skills I could learn. Then Jeff, who I mentioned as well, he was just super technical.

Then outside of the coaching staff, I've gone through a few sports psychologists and I've used strength and conditioning coaches in my time with GB. The ones that really bought into the objectives of the team and who would both ... What would be the word? They would provide check and challenge, but it was always based on the direction we were heading in in the team.

I worked with a few folks who just came in with a mindset that "This is what you needed to do on the strength and conditioning perspective" and "This is what you needed to do psychologically". But it didn't really match the journey we were trying to go in and our objectives.

What also you don't want is somebody who just comes in and agrees with everything that you're doing. It was making sure that we had a nice blend.

I'm smiling a little bit because during my time with GB, we had a statistician who was quite hard work. But when he got his mind to the job, he was brilliant. He was really good. But keeping him on task was just a challenge. What you have to do is, if you're leading a group of staff is, sometimes you have to put up with some people's foibles because they bring something fantastic to the group with their knowledge.

That's taking me back to my time at NUC as well, because we certainly had an interesting stato. I mean, sometimes you just have to ... As long as it doesn't disrupt the group - the harmony in the group - if this person is bringing in something really super, great. But you've got to manage the harmony in the group. Because if somebody is a bit like an outlier, if they're too much of an outlier, the harmony starts to be impacted. That's when it's not a good addition.

But again, somebody who complements what you do and is willing to check and challenge, as well as somebody who gets behind the vision and the objectives.

You mentioned a couple of times in there your stats guys. How have you, in the past, integrated statistics and/or technology into your programs?

That's certainly evolved with the time in the GB program because it was full-time. I remember when I was the England coach for seven years, we had pen and paper and we had video that we just watched and rewound and watched and rewound.

Again, I'm giving away my age, Lauren.

There were those days where you used it in that way. Then all of a sudden DataVolley and DataVideo came in. It was quite a steep learning curve to really understand that system, which I think is brilliant, by the way.

Typically, as a coach, you find a statistical system and you get quite excited about it. Then you overuse it and then you find out over time, you've underused it because it has so many more attributes. I definitely really, really valued it because it allowed you to not only review your team and your team's own performance, but the opposition analysis. I think it's really an important tool.

Now, it's evolved further. People are using it in the game. It wasn't that long ago there were no comms between the bench and the guy on the stato table. Whereas now, there's comms, and there has been for some time. You can get in-the-moment information to the coach on the side or to the people on the bench. I think stats plays a really important part.

But I still use paper stats these days. I mean, with the GB, we had a stato guy with the whole DataVolley and the DataVideo, but we also had the players doing a little bit stats on the side. When they came into a match, they were tuned in. They knew who was passing bad, so they knew that we're going after them from the service line. The setter knew who was hot, so who you wanted to feed, etc., etc. I still, to this day, get players to do a little bit of their own because it helps educate them in volleyball whilst you've got the swanky technology that you can use through video and through computers.

But it's such a big part of sport these days. It's very interesting. I work in football now and I watch in football matches, you have a bench and you have all these guys sitting on the bench, generally with their arms folded. I think, "You've got all of that stuff. Why aren't you utilizing that stuff? Use some kind of statistics." It's slowly changing.

But in volleyball, you just need to look at the US. They've got two people on a headset. They've got two people doing some stats and they're feeding information in. The same as Gio [Giovanni Guidetti, also featured in the first Wizards book] is now in Turkey and was in Italy. He uses stats really, really well. He's got his coaching pad with an iPad on it, so he's getting instant replays of the block that just happened, or whatever. I think it plays a big part.

But my watch out for it is don't get so obsessed with it. Always remember to use your coaching eyes, because stats doesn't tell you about mood, or environment, or what else is going on. I always put a warning triangle next to it. It's really, really vital and important, but don't forget to use your intuition and your coaching eyes.

You've mentioned a couple - which I really appreciate you being so open - but what are some mistakes you've made in the past and things that you've learned or changes you've made from those mistakes?

One I mentioned was at right early doors was, because I'd been pretty successful as an athlete and I had a way of doing things. I thought that was a methodology and that people were all going to be like me. That was definitely a learning that everyone's different and you've got to work out a way to get the best out of people. That was certainly a big piece for me. I have this little cycle thing about, develop your own self-awareness, and once you've got that, you can then have a much better impact on people. Being able to then develop really meaningful relationships and how to get the best out of folk. I've learned that and made mistakes along the way with that.

Then certainly veering from your philosophy. I mentioned that already, that I had a way of doing things and my philosophy about planning, per-severance, belief in people, get you a performance. When you veer from that - and it's good to do that to evolve and try new things - but I learned that veering too far from that took me away from what I stood for and what I believed in and what I thought was really true. I've learned to always check in now with my philosophy and stay true to what I really believe in. I was a serious competitor and a relatively serious coach that learned to enjoy it more. But it was all about getting the best out of people, getting a performance. That was the real joy.

And keeping boundaries between a player and the team. I had really clear boundaries with GB. I had really clear boundaries with the England team. Clubs are different and learning that it is a bit different. I was a club player. I was a club player/coach. Then you transition from being a player into coaching, you develop boundaries.

My advice to anybody is, make sure wherever you go, if you change roles, whether it's going from club to country or a club to another club, just revisit your philosophy and revisit your boundaries. Because you might have to tweak them a little bit, or remember what they are to stay true to yourself. Did I answer the question? I'm not sure.

Absolutely! What are your favorite parts of coaching?

In terms of the actual volleyball piece or just coaching per se?

Just whichever one brings to mind first.

Okay. Well, obviously the setting piece. I love working with setters. Getting them to really, really grasp ...

Obviously there's the technical elements in it, but it's learning how to really orchestrate and run the match. It's like the midfield in football. You're orchestrating what's going on from the defense to the attack. That part of the game I love working with setters on - how we're going to really execute the game plan and get the best out of people. Make the middle block to look really dumb on the other side. That's a passion of mine. I love that opportunity to do that.

Then, again, from my beach days, clearly as you'd imagine at being 5'6" and a bit, I was in the defense. Defense has always been a big part of ...

Again, part of my philosophy. I love working on defense. That came from my very early days from my school coach having gone to Japan. I love Japanese volleyball. I love the way they train. I love the repetition. Taking that into some of my training, I really enjoy and I get joy from seeing other people really enjoying defending. There's nothing better than digging. Somebody's hit the ball so hard and you dig it, that's just an amazing feeling.

That aspect of it, the training of the setter and the training of defense are something that I really, really enjoy. Linked to that is, outwitting your position and seeing a setter do that and seeing her get so excited that she's done that and done that on her own, that's incredibly rewarding, I think, as a coach.

You've moved from coaching. You are still coaching, but your main work is in coach development now. Why did you make that move, and can you talk about what it entails?

When I worked in Volleyball England, one of the key things I wanted to do was to look at how we develop coaches in volleyball. I started off looking at what does the talent look like in England. So who are the coaches that are coming through? It was an element of when a coach is about to move on, have you got talent coming through? That was where my kind of desire to work with coaches came initially to - let's identify who are the talented coaches. Then second to that, how are we going to help them get better? Not just get better about how to teach somebody how to dig, or to set, or to block, or whatever, but also how to coach. How to put on a good practice, session objectives, creating the right environment, engaging with players. All of a sudden, it made me look even deeper into what is coaching? What is coaching all about? Because people tend to just think of the tech[nical], tact[tical] stuff. There's so much more to coaching practice.

That really started to whet my appetite. I started doing that at Volleyball England. I then went to work for UK Coach and started working with athletes who were transitioning into coaching. Having had that experience myself, and knowing the journey and the steps that take. As an athlete, you'll know yourself, you know it, but then you've got to translate that and interpret it now as a coach. Because you'll have your way of thinking and learning, but players think and learn differently to you. The skill is how to do that as a coach with different players.

It started off looking for talented coaches, then really getting underneath what is coaching all about outside of the technical, tactical piece. Now, I find myself working in football. I was attracted to that because women's football was taking off and I was also attracted to it to look at how do we get more women into coaching. Because being in football is male dominated. There was a real opportunity there to look at how do we develop coaches to make them better? How do we get more female coaches? That was a big motivation for the work I'm currently doing in coach development.

As I said, really, I'm picking, what is coaching? What is coaching all about? How do you coach outside of, and including the technical, tactical aspects of coaching? Because clearly I'm not an expert in football technical and tact, but I love the game and I understand it. I have a team of people that are footballers and are now coaches. But what we focus on is, what's the craft of coaching? That's the bit that I get really excited about in terms of helping in developing coaches.

Yeah, I think there needs to be a bit more of this kind of role across Europe, honestly. You mentioned female coaches. This moves on to the next part of the interview. It's a series targeted at female coaches. We're pretty underrepresented in Europe. What are some of the barriers to females getting into coaching at a high level?

I think there's definitely still a cultural piece, Lauren, around women in coaching. Even to the extent of, "Can women coach?" Of course they can coach. But if they're not seen to coach, then people can assume that they can't coach. From sports that are male dominated they've not seen very many female coaches. Some of the barriers are perception technically from male dominated environments.

Also, the perception that may ... I guess it takes you back to the days of autocratic type coaching. I remember the days of Karpol. He's a famous Russian coach, but he was very dictatorial very often - incredibly so. That was deemed as what coaching was all about. But a modern day coach doesn't look like that. If you take somebody like Karch [Kiraly], they couldn't be further apart. Lang Ping couldn't be further apart from that way of coaching. It was seen as you had to be a male and you had to be dominant and so forth. That was what coaching was all about, but coaching has changed.

I think the perception of what you need to look like and sound like is different now. One, I think there are more opportunities for women now. But some organizations still see coaching a little bit like that, and they don't believe that women have the same traits to be able to be authoritative. But coaching isn't all about cracking the whip and saying, "It's my way or the highway." Females bring so many great natural interpersonal skills into coaching that I think we're missing an opportunity, really missing an opportunity.

Generally speaking, females - and I'm talking female sport and sort of coaching female volleyballers - we understand women. I always think we should have way more coaches in women's sport. Having them in women's sport will open the door into male sport because we need role models. There aren't that many great role models. The work I do now is, "Let's get them in at grassroots level, at the early stages". Moms are taking their girls or their boys to their sport. Get them involved in coaching in some way. Ex-players, let's get them into coaching. Let's see whether it's something that they would find rewarding.

Then there's, of course, as females, we're not very good at putting ourselves forward. We tend to not have massive egos. We're not that great ... I'm stereotyping a little bit now, but research has shown that we, as females do not put ourselves forward. I mean, there's quite a lot of statistics being done around, if a job is up on the internet and you look at that job and you go through it as a female and we go, "Okay, I've looked at the specification. I've looked at the essentials and the desirables. I can do about 50% of that. I'm pretty confident I'm not applying." A bloke would look at it, and they go, "Yeah, I can do that. Not so good at that. Probably about 50%. I'm applying." There's research being done on this. We're not that great as females at putting ourselves forward. Part of that is we have to work with young girls and females early doors to build their confidence and to understand the strengths that they bring to coaching.

I've just done a whole load of research here in England, around what is effective coaching in women's football. We asked players, what does effective coaching look like? Then, through that research, we found out what they said about what females bring to coaching. They're equally proficient at the technical and tactical side, but they bring all this other stuff that they understand you, they understand how you tick, they bring that kind of empathetic side to it, as well as being able to lay the law down when they need to. But they do that in a way that's constructive.

I think females have a lot of attributes that are underplayed because we're thinking too much about, "I don't have this." Or, "I don't have that." We can be, in many senses, our own worst enemy. Some of the work I do is about creating many opportunities for female only courses and opportunities and programs where we target females. We've created a pool of talented female coaches that we're going to wrap around some support with. Because what females also want is to feel valued and to feel supported.

That's just a need that we have. In the female race, there are things that are dead important to us. If we have that, we can excel. What I'm trying to do in football is make sure that we provide that support for female coaches in order to excel.

I use a phrase, Lauren, about nudging. We nudge them. Sometimes we just need a little gentle push as a female. Yes, you can do that. Yes, you are good. Yes, apply for that job. We use that term of nudging, a little gentle nudge from a mentor for somebody saying, "Yes, you can. Let's talk about what you're really good at." Then there's a lifestyle thing of being a professional coach.

I think, again, back in the old days, the woman stayed at home and looked after the children and the men went out to work. Well, that's not the modern age these days. I think there are more opportunities.

It's difficult because a female is often associated with bringing up the children, but I think as an employer we have to be more flexible. Whether you're a club chair or you're a national governing body, how can we be flexible to allow females to travel and to look after ... Part of their role was to look after children if they had kids. There's lots of aspects to it, but we have to be proactive. We can't just expect it to happen because I think we've been expecting it to happen for too long.

I feel like I've gone on a soap box because I feel so passionate about this part. The statistics at the Olympics - I think the last four Olympics - it's ranged from 9% to 10% of head coaches are female. It hasn't changed in 16 years because we've not done enough. We've not been proactive enough. We've not nudged enough. We've not talked about the qualities that females bring to coaching and how coaching has changed. We need to talk up about that way more to really champion females as coaching. It pains me that there still aren't more female volleyball coaches at the top end. Because they're women out there that we need to nudge them and help them to get on that journey to be a successful professional coach and a national team coach. But we have to provide them with support, either as an employer or as a developer of coaches.

Sorry, I feel like I should be quiet now because I'll keep talking about it. Because it's such a big piece, Lauren, that you're a role model. How much do you talk about what you're doing? You're a professional coach. Even just seeing your face now, we probably don't. I mean, I'd love to do a story on you to tell the volleyball community about you as a coach. We need to tell these stories, that it is possible and that women are really good at coaching.

You absolutely crushed all my questions, but I'm going to try and ask another one and see if I can get you back on the soap box because I really, really want to talk about this as much as possible. If there was a stereotype or misunderstanding of female coaches that you would want to clear up around you against, what would it be? It can be more than one.

I probably mentioned a few in that piece there. The one that frustrates me the most is around that women don't have the same technical and tactical ability. It's so not true. There are so many incredible strategists in business [who are] female, and there are presidents now in the world. Women have an incredible ability to think outside the box and be statisticians, and strategize, and theorize and so forth. I think there's a myth that men do that better than women, and I just really don't think that's true.

I also don't think it's true that women are soft. That bugs me - that women are soft and men are hard. That is not true. There are men who are incredibly empathetic and there are women that can really be challenging, but do it in the right way to get the best out of people.

There are things that do frustrate me that where we... I'd done it tonight. I've stereotyped a bit. But when we do that to the extreme, and pigeonhole people, and pigeonhole women, that they're really not that capable of doing it, that frustrates me. There are some incredible women. In volleyball terms, Lang Ping is certainly one of the most successful. Who is the other female coach in Switzerland that used to coach at Volero?

Svetlana Ilic.

Is she still coaching?

She is still coaching and at Volero. They're back in Switzerland.

Okay. Again, she has a style which has her style. She's probably a little bit more on the hard side, but I bet she knows how to get the best out of some of those female players. Sometimes we forget to play up those really super attributes that we have. We can be stern, we can be challenging, but equally we know how to find other ways of getting the best out of people.

I use this phrase of dialing things up and dialing them down. Sometimes we need to dial up some of those strengths and overplay them a little bit more and show that we're as capable and equal as men in coaching.

Going a little bit back to the how, you talked about part of your role is to bring more females into coaching in football. How is that supposed to be implemented on a bigger scale in volleyball in Europe? It's just not even thought of. It's not even talked about. Not even a little bit in federation.

I think we do need to talk about it within the federations. I think looking at the gender split in terms of the amount of coaches, I think we have to be proactive, Lauren. I think we can't just wait for it to happen. I think that's what federations do, they wait for it to happen. They say, "Well, we're making it available." But often, that old phrase that you have to lead a horse to water, we sometimes have to do a little bit more to lead the horse to water and actually help them show them how to drink it. That's a horrible phrase, but in Europe, we have to really be proactive. I think we need to do that and we need to chime in and we need to talk about those values. I don't think there's enough going on. There's not enough proactiveness going on.

I actually look at myself, and I sit on the FIVB Coaching commission, and I haven't pushed it anywhere near as hard as I should. But if I'm still on that group going forward, I'm absolutely going to be having that on the agenda. Because I think as an international federation we don't even talk about it so much. I think we do need to talk about it. We need to have it on the agenda.

Female coaches, and we call it BAME coaches -Black, Asian, and minority ethnic coaches - here in England, is another focus area for us. There are areas that we're really putting a lot of attention to so that the playing demographic and the population is ...

What is it? 49/51?

Our coaching split is 90/10, or in some respects, much higher than that. We have to do something proactively to change the dial. I think national governing bodies have a responsibility to do that. We need to promote and we need to talk about good role models. A good way to do it is to put in player-to-coach programs. It's a really super methodology to take players who are coming to the end of their career, or who get injured, and start to work with them around helping them transition into coaching. The earlier we can do that, I think we'll then get a bigger swell of female coaches.

At grassroots levels, moms take their kids, they drive them to the sports' hall. Get them to do a little bit of stuff, a little bit of coaching, a little bit something on the side that resembles coaching just to help kids have fun playing volleyball, and see who has an appetite and who enjoys doing that. There's different ways that we can do that, but we have to proactively do it. We can't just hope that it will happen. Sometimes it needs people to champion it. I think of myself as a champion in that. It often needs a champion within a club or within a national governing body to say, "I'm going to do something about this." Then other people suddenly join in. But you need somebody to really champion it.

Before we move on topics, I'm not ready to go yet, and have there been any challenges that you faced that are unique to female coaches? Any examples?

Yeah. I mean, to be honest, again, I'll be very candid with you. When I was a GB coach, I often felt that my male equivalent got what he wanted. One, because he shouted loud and that the management were male. Therefore, there was a bond in a way, if you like. This actually comes back to one of your earlier questions - what were some of my learnings as a coach? Is to influence upwards. I didn't do that well enough. I didn't influence upwards enough to be able to talk about what I needed and what was important to me as a national team coach for the women, and that we saw that the women were treated equally to the men.

An answer to your question, I've definitely experienced that as a female - that whoever shouts loudest and if your voice isn't heard, they'll just forget about it. I think you've got to make sure you have a voice at the table in order to do that. It's just one aspect of it.

Any others? I mean, there's a funny one.

It's actually where my Twitter handle came about. I remember we went to the Dominican with the GB team and we were on the coach [bus]. The guy who was looking after us came in and there was a male head coach at the time, Lorne, from Canada. He knew who Lorne was. Then I think he thought I was a physio because I was a female. That usual thing. Then he realized I was the assistant coach, and I let him know that quite politely. Then he started calling me lady coach, "Lady coach. Lady coach." I took that as it was meant. It was not trying to be derogatory, but it was just, "It's a lady coach." That's where my Twitter handle came from. But I could have been really offended by it.

I've spoken to many coaches who've walked into a sport or in football where they just assume, because you're a female, you're the doctor or the physio. I think that's really quite insulting for females. I've experienced that a little bit.

I can't count the amount of times that the referees have gone straight to my assistant to talk to them, and I'm like, "It's me. I'm the head coach."

There's just this thing, Lauren. People in their minds think my point earlier: it's a team, it's a coach, it's got to be a man, isn't it? Yeah. What we're trying to change is people's perceptions and it's the systemic piece that they just assume that it's males that are the coaches. You're making changes by being the head coach and people realizing.

Thank you for that. That was great. I really believe we can't be what we can't see. There are more women in this position and there's not going to be any women coming through. Thank you for trying to make a change in our sport there.

Last two questions. A totally different topic now. Reading list, do you have any books that you can recommend or that you would recommend?

One of my early ones was Covey's book, *The 7 Habits of Effective People*. Being a little bit processy and anal, that was really good, but it just really taught me about what the good things are as a leader.

Then there's another book called *Bounce*, which is all about identifying talent and how to look for talent.

They're probably the ones that stand out. There's one at the moment I'm reading, it's called *Rebels* and it's by Matthew Syed. It's about leadership and it's all around cognitive diversity. A little bit like I was talking about before. If you just bring people around you that are like you, you're going to miss loads of opportunity. This is one that I'm kind of working my way through at the moment about making sure you've got cognitive diversity. When you asked about staff, making sure that you've got people who think a little bit different to you, and maybe got a different perspective and can bring that in. Matthew Syed is an author that writes a few books on sport that I would recommend. He's written a few. A couple of names escape me at the moment. But as an author, I would look him up in terms of a book.

Great! Surprisingly, so many people don't have answers to that question. I appreciate that we have a few books there for people to read.

To finish up, do you have any advice for coaches just starting their career?

General advice would be, starting their career, get to know yourself and what you stand for. Really develop your level of self-awareness and continuously ... I use this phrase, hold up the mirror. Look at yourself. Look at who you are, what you stand for, how you're behaving. Because once you know yourself really, really well, you'll understand the impact you can have on others. Then you'll start to understand others and how they're the same as you and different to you.

Within all of that, you're developing and learning what coaching and coaching practice is all about. As young coaches, when you say to a young coach, "How would you like to develop?" "I'd like to go and watch. I'd like to go and watch Lauren coaching because she's a professional coach." Of course, we like to go and watch coaches who we aspire to be, and that's a great way to learn. They also want to go and learn about the technical and tactical side, but they forget to learn about all those other aspects about how do you engage players. How do you create the right environment? You've got to know self to get to know others. Really get to know and understand yourself. Develop your level of self-awareness to really then be successful as a coach. It's a bit like, you can tell after you've coached for a while you learn that and you go, "Wow, I'd be great if I knew that when I was younger. "

The other piece of advice is get different views and different perspectives on things. Because we've all got biases. Everyone has biases. It's good for those biases to be checked and challenged.

Then the third one is, get a good mentor. Get a really good mentor.

Chapter Four

Ann Schilling

Ann Shilling, from the U.S., is the extremely successful coach of Bayside Academy at the high school level in Alabama. She has 28 state titles and more than 1500 victories to her credit in her 30+ years at the school. At publication they are on a streak of 21 consecutive state championships. She was selected as the 2009 Prep Volleyball Co-National Coach of the Year and the 2011 National Federation of High Schools' National Coach of the Year. In 2018 Ann was inducted into the Alabama High School Athletic Association Hall of Fame, and in 2021 she was inducted into the Alabama High School Coaches Association Hall of Fame. Her battle with breast cancer saw her receive the 2019 Sports Imports/AVCA Courage Award. In this interview, she talks a lot about her philosophy, how her approach has changed over the years, and how she keeps learning and stays motivated. She also shares how her journey in dealing with cancer has changed her perspective on life and coaching.

***

Could you please start by telling us about your history and experience in volleyball? How did you get here and about your journey in general?

I started playing in fifth grade in a Catholic parochial league in Mobile, Alabama. Then went on to play in high school. Then from there I had opportunities to go play volleyball and basketball, and I chose basketball. I went to Auburn University. They did not have a volleyball team at that point. My fifth year, they reinstated the volleyball program. I was asked to help out. It's probably one of the best decisions I made. I played, and I never lost the love of it. After that, my high school coach's husband called. He was at a small private school in Daphne, Alabama - Bayside Academy. He called me and he said, "We have an opening if you come interview for it." Here I am getting ready to start my 34th year at the same place.

Do you want to just let us know a little bit of the successes you've had. I have read them, but it would be great to hear.

We have a small streak of 18 in a row state championships right now. We've won 25 since I've arrived at the school. The school has 28 state championships. I have three runner up trophies. I mean, we've had a bevy of success; have a lot of kids who have gone on to the next level, whether it be [NCAA] Division III, Division II, or Division I. It's been a great ride.

I'm not from America, so I don't very well know the high school system. I understand that you guys have won in several divisions.

Yes. We started out in 1A, and then we moved to 2A. Then we moved to 3A. There's a rule called competitive balance, and the multiplier that they instituted is basically why we went to 3A. Then, the competitive balance rule pushed us to 4A. Then next year we'll play 5A. There's seven divisions, just to give you an idea. If we were not a private school, and we weren't under all these restrictions, we would be a 2A school. We're going to play three levels up this year, which is fine with us. We like the challenge. It's kind of fun actually. Just tell your kids, hey, we could get five. Five different levels of championships this year if we can do it. [Bayside went on not only to win the 5A title, but then the 6A in 2022]

For those of us that don't know too much about the high school system, could you tell us a little bit what a week looks like for your athletes.

Preseason, mid season, end of season, all of it?

Yeah. Just like a general week with classes and training.

In our school, we do not have any kind of weight training for the girls. What we do is during the season two days a week, just depending on when our matches are. We'll work out from 6:15-7:15. They'll shower, go to school, come in the gym. We'll practice from 3:30-5:30.

Does that change in those phases that you said? Preseason, in season, things like that or it's…

Yeah. Preseason we'll go four days a week of workouts. Then weight workouts. Then once we start the season we'll go to two. Sometimes if we play a lot, we'll go just to one. Just depending on the amount of matches that we play. Summer right now, we have practice four days a week and workout four days a week. Right now I'm pretty much letting them on their own because we're having to wear masks when we go in the gym.

On a normal year, we'd workout four days a week and once the season starts, we'll cut it back to two. After our season ends at the beginning of November, we will take off until January the following year and then start back up four days a week. Then, they'll go into club and all that.

All right, could you tell us about some coaching influences that you've had over the years.

The first one I have to name was my high school coach, Becky Dickinson. She coached me for four years. When I got the job, she was an ear that I bended all the time. Just a lot of back and forth, a lot of feedback. I asked her about a lot of different things. A lot of different scenarios, stuff that I had forgotten. Just advice. How to handle mostly just different situations.

I pick a lot of people's brains. Melissa Walters at the University West Florida, she's one. Ruth Nelson, Penny Lucas-White, Shawn Taylor who's coaching beach now at Southern Miss. I just have a bevy of coaches, and a bunch of high school coaches. We all pick each other's brains. I think it's a real healthy situation with the high school coaches too. I mean we're all competitive, but we all have a lot of respect for each other. We just pick each other's brains and talk a lot of volleyball.

How has your coaching philosophy changed over time?

At first, I was probably a dictatorship a lot. There wasn't a lot going on right I don't think. Just got kind of lucky. The kids kind of put up with me. Now, it's more about building relationships with the athletes. You find out that you can be hard on them if they know you care. Thing about it is I don't ever want to run anybody away or turn anybody off of the sport. I want them to love it as much as I do. That's my philosophy.

At first, I don't think I really understood the relationship part of things as much as I should have. I guess I was so busy trying to draw that line because I was young and they were young. You don't forget, but you just don't do what you probably needed to do most. I made a lot of errors. I made a lot of mistakes. If I didn't know something, instead of asking somebody, I'd probably make something up just to prove that I knew it. I think now I just want to know more, want to find out. Picking each other's brains, like I said. It's a lot of fun. I just enjoy what I do so much. Just so grateful for the opportunity to do it.

To put it very black and white, what do you think made you make that change, or what realizations did you find?

Just watching other coaches. Just observing. I tell you, I walked on to the basketball team at Auburn. I really learned a lot because I sat a lot. I learned a lot by sitting there and watching. I didn't at first put it into what I was doing. I was just flying by the seat of my pants. Once you stop and think, though... just thinking about those days and talking to people; watching, like I said. I watched a lot. Just figured out what worked - what responded best with my teams and my kids.

You just said you were watching the basketball team. Did you find the benefits in watching coaches from different sports as well?

Yes. I watch a lot of different coaches coach a lot of different sports - especially the successful ones - to try to see what they're doing and why they're successful. I try to hopefully put some of those things into action.

They could be from other coaching in general rather than just volley- ball coaching as itself?

Absolutely. It is an art.

Moving on to training methodology, are there differences between a training session from now and from when you started coaching?

Yeah, drastic.

What are some examples?

Just a lot of block training. We were pretty bad. Of course, back then I thought we were pretty good. We were really bad. The skills were just not there. The training now is just so much more intense than it was back then. Back then, it was just a lot of block training. Maybe 6-on-6 the last 15 minutes when we would scrimmage, or something like that. There's a lot more technical, a lot more tactical now. Just different things that we've put into play. As I've learned to be a better coach, my practices have been a lot better.

Yeah. I haven't been coaching that long, but if I go back to my first training session, it's a lot different.

It would be really scary. It'd be kind of funny if you could get a lot of people. I've talked to a lot of people. When it's 33 years ago, that's a long time ago.

It's a different culture.

It's a whole different game. Totally different game.

You've obviously created a winning culture, which has transcended through multiple divisions as well. Can you talk a little bit about what goes into that and how you achieved it.

I think success breeds success. Once my kids... They have a lot of ownership in the program and they are very proud of it. They do a lot of the grunt work. Showing the ropes to the younger kids. The younger kids - even though you have some kids that aren't real talented - just being a part of something successful, they feel it. They really play at a higher level and play harder. I think just that one thing, that they want to be good. They want to spend the time. You'll have average kids play above average, and just being part of the program. Like I said, success brings success. Nobody wants to be that first group that goes down. I mean, it's going to happen. They don't want to be that team. I think that's what really motivates them a lot as well too. Along with the fact that they enjoy working with each other, working together on the team.

I think the culture in our gym... A college coach came and did a little 2-day camp. She said, she'd been to over 40 camps that year. She said, "You know, the culture in your gym is better than any other culture of any other high school that I've ever worked with." I just took that as a huge, huge, huge compliment. Because she sees something that's different in our gym that's not in others. I think it's the hard work and just the... The kids are... It's amazing some of the things that they're doing, but it's not without a lot of blood, sweat, and tears.

I have a couple questions out of that. You said that the girls take a lot of ownership in the culture. Would you be able to give us some examples of how you implemented that and how you give them ownership over this?

I listen a lot more than I used to. I think that was one of the mistakes early on that I didn't listen enough. I ask them things like, how are your legs? How are your arms today? How do you feel today? Just things like that. I think they know that I care about how they feel so that we can stay injury free. They have ownership in our team-building stuff. They do a lot of that. They create things that they want to do. They come back to the coaching staff and say, "Hey, this is what we want to do." We approve it. We may give them a couple of ideas to go along with it. When you give kids ownership that they feel so much more a part of it. They're going to work that much harder for the program.

Would you have some examples of some things that you might have done in the past in terms of team-building.

They do more of go out to eat together. We do tie-dyed shirts. After practice, they'll tie-dye t-shirts and then they'll wear them the next day. They'll go out to breakfast in the morning after workouts, if they have time. Usually more in the summer. They've done that a couple of times here lately. It doesn't always have to be your traditional team-building things. It's simple stuff. It's just spending time together and talking and coming up with...

Three of them came over to my house a couple of days ago. We talked about a lot of things. I asked them what they envisioned. What do they see? What do they want to do? I asked them a lot of questions about what do they see. How can we all work together? I think those are some of the things they do all the time. They do spend a lot of time together.

You said that no group wants to be the group that doesn't win. That's a lot of repeated success. How do you address expectations and handling pressure with your athletes?

You know they feel it. You know that's going on. I tell you one thing. My stud player used to be an example. She's an outside hitter. We were just having a team meeting. She started to tear up. This was about two weeks before the season was over. She said, "I just feel such pressure". My whole team kind of stopped and they looked at her. I thought that was huge that she said that because a lot of kids would just keep that under wraps - fake it; act like everything's okay. What it did was give all those kids an avenue.

We started talking about how we could help. How can we take some of that pressure off of her, and how can we help her not to feel that. It was so key. I try to crack a couple of jokes right before we play. Just stay calm and know that we're all going to wake up the next day, win or lose.

I've seriously had players throw up after the state championship match, which I don't really want. I haven't had it lately. That was after seven. We kind of figured out ways to relax them. I try to put the pressure on them in practice so that when they play in that big match [they're ready]. I know there's no way you can emulate that much pressure, but I'll do things to put a lot of pressure on them in practice so that they feel it a lot there. Then the games will be a little bit easier.

What kind of things? Would you be able to expand on that?

We'll do little mini games, and it'll be a serve receive game. The starting side will have like 21 and the other side will have 23. They get a first ball kill is two points. If it's a transition side out, they get one. If it's too easy, I'll make the score a little bit farther apart. Just do things like that. They have to do something if they lose. Just try to make them feel that pressure as much as possible. That's one thing we do.

What about playing time issues? I'm always interested to hear how do you keep non-starters engaged. Are you playing them the same?

Well, usually it's not the kid. It's more the parent at the high school level. The beauty about our program is we're successful and I never cut anybody. Everybody gets an opportunity. I have given some of those bench kids, or the kids that don't play as much, [a role]. I have control of that bench. I tell them, "Hey, you're here to keep the energy up". You just try to do things to help those kids feel more a part of things. Usually those kids have a role. I have kids that come in and just serve. It's hard to convince those kids, "Hey, you're just going to do this". If you tell them how important, it is and how much they mean to the team. I think they're going to embrace it. I've found that a lot of times it's more the parent than the kid that's upset. I try to tell them, "If you just don't think you can be happy, this is probably not the right team for you".

Do the girls that come to you have aspirations of playing college volleyball?

Yeah. We've probably had, gosh, I don't even know how many. Just at different levels. I got one going to a great school – a Division II school. She could have gone Division I, but she is going to a great D2 institution about an hour away. She didn't want to go too far away. If they want to play, a lot of them get that opportunity. I mean there's always college coaches that want kids, especially from a successful program, because they know how to win.

What's your role in that?

I'll do whatever it takes. I got a phone call yesterday about one of my rising juniors. I mean, I'll help them in any way. Some of them sign up with one of those scouting people that help them. I can help them do their filming. Whatever I need to do, I'll help them do. That's kind of my role.

Changing topics a little, what about leadership and captain selection? How do you select team captains and what are their responsibilities?

Well, we kind of take it as a job interview. They have a list of things that they have to understand if they want to apply. I make them get 2-3 recommendations. It can't be any family members. They have to get a recommendation from a club coach. It could be a teacher. Whoever. I need two or three. They get up and kind of give a little speech to the team. Then, the kids vote on it. The coaches, we all vote as well. That's the way we do it most years.

Do a lot of kids apply?

Last year, I think I had every single kid on my team except for one. It got whittled down pretty fast. It was pretty obvious. I think everybody gets excited at first. Once they see a couple of them just go over the top, then they realize that, "Hey, these two really need to be it".

What are the roles of your captains?

Just managing the team. They are to deal with the issues first. Team rules like no drinking, no smoking. They just make sure that none of those rules are being violated. Academically that everybody's doing what they need to do. Golly, there's more. I have a list, but I don't have it in front of me. I have about eight things that they have to do. And respect everybody. That's a big one. The respect is huge in our program.

Does that go well every year - the people the girls vote for you would agree with? Or is there ups and downs with that?

There's ups and downs with that. There's been ups and downs. The coaching staff has picked some years because there's been years that we've felt like the ones they picked just weren't the right ones. We kind of stepped in and did our part. No, it doesn't always go well. Some years, it's just a matter of you don't really have a clear leader or two. Those are years where you may give different responsibilities - just one responsibility to four or five different kids. We've done that just because there's no clear person that's just going to [take charge]. I think sometimes when it's a younger kid, you know that they're going to be the one that are leading your team. You know that they aren't going to be the ones that are going to get voted for. That's kind of tricky too. Sometimes we just kind of give four or five different things to do. Let that one do her job, and the other ones seem to be happy because they feel like they're a part of it.

How many captains do you have? I didn't ask that earlier.

We usually have two - sometimes three, sometimes we have one. Just depending on the makeup of our team. How many kids are there? It just depends. One to three, but no more than three.

Do they do any weekly meetings together or with you?

They do. This past year our two captains did a phenomenal job. They met with the team probably once a week just to make sure everybody's on the same page. As you know, coaching girls can be challenging at times. They really kept the drama down. They did a phenomenal job.

I like that idea about the job applications. I haven't heard that before. Did you come up with that yourself?

No, no. All of my ideas are stolen. All of them are stolen.

You said you were constantly striving to learn. As someone who's had honestly unprecedented success at this level. How do you ensure that you keep learning?

I mean, you've got to. I think volleyball changes. It changes drastically even from year to year. I mean, it's just you're always challenged to keep learning. If you're kind of stagnant, that's not how I roll. I just want to keep getting better. My kids get better. I attend clinics. I bend a lot of coach's ears. I'll go watch college practices. Every level. I'll go watch club practices just to see what people are doing. I love to watch people coach. I love to watch in match and in practice. I love both of them. I just strive to be a better coach every year.

I think that's quite important, just watching other coaches do their craft and sort of taking what applies to you as a coach and what's authentic to you.

Yeah, and you can learn a lot about yourself. There's a lot of things that I've learned from people I saw like this. It's like, I didn't even realize I was doing it. It would be something small. That's the thing. If you watch, you can really notice a lot of things about all the coaches and really learn a lot.

Absolutely. As coaches we need to be pretty knowledgeable in a lot of areas, whether it be technical, tactical, or personal. What do you think the most important qualities to coaching are?

That is a loaded question. Golly. Of course you got to have all of them.

I think one of the biggest compliments that I get about our team is that the kids they play so doggone hard. Technically, tactically, I think we're sound in both of those things. At the end of the day, I think that's one of the reasons why we have been so successful. Is because when the lights come on, the kids are going to play hard and they're not going to give up. We're going to be relentless and we're not going to quit. I think probably that part is the biggest thing, and just having fun. If it's not fun, then I'm not doing a good job of coaching. Because I see some people coach, and the kids are like robots. They don't look like they're having a bit of fun. I think that's where we miss the mark sometimes in our coaching. You got to have it all. I think that the having fun part, and the energy, and all those things, are the most important thing.

It's not the ability to get the players...

Yeah. I mean, it's like I said. It's all important. We do technical stuff too, but I've seen teams that are robotic and the kids are miserable. I'm going, "What in the world is that coach...?" You can learn from those coaches too because they look miserable. They're not smiling. They're not having any fun. Like I said, at the end of the day, I don't ever want to turn anybody off from playing a sport that I love to coach.

I like that. I think that's very important honestly at any level.

I'd like to talk about coaching, and preparations, and training versus match coaching. What do you find to be more important and why?

Well, I think your practice time you try to coach to prepare your kids for every single scenario. What we do is we play tough matches right away because what happens is you get exposed. You figure out real fast. You might not see your weaknesses in practice that [appear] when you start playing teams that are better than you. You get exposed a little bit. Then it enables you to go back to the drawing board, work on those things, and gradually get yourself better.

In matches sometimes I can look like a genius. Sometimes you put a kid in and they miss their serve, shank five... You know what I mean? It's just the nature of that. Mainly what we try to do is it's all about match-up's - just trying to match up our strengths on their weaknesses. You're going to know your weaknesses because they've already gotten exploited. We're just trying to figure out how to neutralize those and then exploit theirs. Sometimes it's hard, especially at a small school. There's sometimes we'll have three really good players and three just kind of okay kids. You can't let those three okay kids get exploited. It's difficult.

But I like both, and a lot of people just like the games. I happen to love practices. I love them. I love games too. We have a philosophy. You bust your tail in practice, and games are a lot more fun. We bust our butts, and work really hard, and then the games are a lot more fun.

You just mentioned the working with match-ups and things like that in a game. What kind of work do you do with the athletes in terms of scouting the opposition?

Well, a lot of kids they'll know... They all play club together. They'll know kids' favorite shots. All you have to do is ask them. Early season, I depend a lot on them to tell me a little bit. I watch a lot of club as well. I run a club, so I see some things. After you play them, if you know you're going to play them again, there's a lot of film watching. We can prepare a lot better after we play them and then we have film. If it's a 3-out-of-5 you got a decent amount of time to make some adjustments. For 2-out-of-3 it's a little bit different story.

We see film and I'll cut out excerpts. They watch film mostly themselves. They'll have the ability to get on a site that we have, and they can watch film. We'll talk about things - what they see, what I saw. What another coach on our staff says. There's a lot of interaction that way.

You guys don't sit together and do team video as much?

We do, but we've done a lot less of that because our time is so limited. I tell them to go watch on their own, and things to look for. I ask them things. It seems to go a lot better because when you have a group something will happen. Somebody will trip in a match or something. Kind of fall over, and they're all laughing. It just becomes a comedy show. I think it really works out better. We do a little bit, but we do far less team than the other. More team during the end of the year most likely.

Do the girls need to watch themselves? Do you do any video on yourselves with the players after games or anything like that?

Yeah. They watch... You mean watch themselves play?

Yeah, like review the game a little bit.

Yeah. We'll talk about a lot of things that happened. If we lost, we're going to learn from that. There's not a loss that we haven't learned a lot of things from. Then, we'll work on those things in practice. Try to not let those things happen again so some other team gets the feeling that they can beat you that way too.

What about integrating statistics and technology beyond what we just talked about now. Do you have any other examples?

Not really. I've got two assistant coaches. They don't get into the gym until about 30-45 minutes after practice has started so it's basically just me. I'll do a little filming on my iPad. Just technical things so that they can see it. We'll do things like that. Basically, that's it.

I do have one of those radars, those pocket radars. We have what's called a solar spy. It's not really technology. You put the ball on it and hit out of the thing. We use that quite a bit. I do use the iPad a lot and film. Especially the younger kids when you're trying to get them to do something different than what they're doing. We definitely do that so you can say, "See what you are doing?"

How long do you have players for? What age do they come into your team and how long do you have them for?

Well, I run a club. They're not all my kids. We start at 8-9 years old. We have a youth development league which starts in second grade. I see athletes anywhere from second, third, on up. Most of them I'm probably going to see fifth or sixth grade on up. Some of them will transfer in during eighth or seventh grade. We'll always have a kid or two that might come because they're not happy where they are. They got cut from their high school team, or whatever.

You have them a long time basically for the most part.

I have them a long time. Yes, I do. Most of them I have a long time.

You mentioned you have two assistant coaches, do you choose them, or are they given to you?

Yeah, I've had the same one for … she's been with me over 15 years. Her daughter, who played for me, just joined our coaching staff a couple years ago. I just hired actually another former player of mine. She's going to be there more than either one of them. They're both elementary school teachers, so that's part of my problem in that they don't get into the gym until probably 45 minutes after practice started. They do a phenomenal job though. It is challenging at times in that setting.

Do you give them specific roles?

Yeah, we do position training. We'll have everybody take a different position and do training like that. In a match, one of them actually takes stats a lot. She kind of peers up and down a little bit. The other one, I'll say maybe I'll give her, "You watch what they're doing and see if we can find any tendencies". I'm kind of watching more of us. That's the way we roll. I'll have an additional person this year, so that'll be a nice thing. We can get a little bit more creative in what we're doing.

What's your vision on your responsibilities with your extra staff member this season?

She was an incredible defensive player. I'm probably just going to unleash her on the defensive side of things. Let her run that. With some feedback.

What are your favorite parts of coaching? What keeps you going?

The relationships with the athletes, with the girls. Just getting to know a different group every year. It's a different group. [Even when] you have the same kids. I can tell you this. You learn something different every year about the same kids. That to me is walking in and seeing them and seeing them succeed. Just having an impact on their lives. Making sure that teaching them life-long skills. A lot of them have grown up to be great nurses and mothers and doctors and lawyers. They come back and they tell you, "Golly, the things that I learned by playing volleyball. It made me who I am today". That, really to me, is the best part of my job. That's what I love. I love having an impact on their lives year after year.

Now you've been at the same place for quite a long time. I guess you've been quite successful in that regard to want to stay there.

Right.

You mentioned a little earlier a couple of examples. What are some mistakes you've made - things you've learned, or changes you've made?

Not listening enough. Being very hard-headed.

I'm extremely competitive. I have my assistant coach ... she is the polar opposite of me. We work very well together because she'll actually say, "Hey, you're being too hard on them. You got to ease up." Just give me a little reality kick in the butt. She's been very helpful because if I didn't have her saying those things, I'm not sure what I would have done. I probably would have run a lot more kids off. Just being too hard. Not listening enough.

Changing my philosophy.

Early on, I didn't know who I was. It probably took me about eight years to figure that out. I would suggest just know who you are. Know who you are, and stick by it. Hire somebody that is not like you. That has been key for me - hiring somebody that is the opposite of you, because you need those people. It's a great situation because some of the things I need to hear she tells me. Sometimes it's hard to listen to. I listen to her a lot.

Did you set that precedent with her when she came that she should challenge you on things that she didn't agree with and things like that?

No, she just did it. We are the same age. We played each other in high school. We knew each other very well. No, she just started doing it. At first, I got angry. Then I started really looking in the mirror and go, "Hey, you do need to tone it down a little bit". My feelings were hurt at first, but then I knew it was... We talked and she said, "Look, I'm just trying to help you with some constructive criticism." I didn't take it to heart. I took it, and I was like, "She's right". I changed. That was a blessing.

That's amazing. Okay. If you're open to it, I'd really like to discuss your journey with the cancer.

Yeah.

Would you be able to tell us the timeline? Diagnosis and things like that.

January of 2018, end of January I was diagnosed with breast cancer. Then, about mid-February we figured out it was stage four to the liver. March, or end of February I started chemo. My doctor even called me up. My liver was terrible. I mean it was awful. He had a poker face on. He didn't want to tell me how bad it was. I was pretty bad.

Anyway, after three rounds, he called excited. He said, "Some of this cleared up. Over 50% of your tumors are gone." He said, "We're going to do three more." I did a PET scan and I just had one really small spot. They were talking about doing a liver abrasion, because they didn't think they were going to be able to get it all before that. Long story short, I got another PET scan after probably about 9-10 months. My liver was totally clear. Then I went and got a mastectomy.

Then about two weeks ago, just for my peace of mind. I got a full hysterectomy and my left breast removed. I think the results that I had were incredible. I think one of my doctor's said there's a less than 1% chance - that what happened to me with my liver is one of the hardest places to clear. It cleared up. I just had a huge journey of faith. I never did miss a practice. I never missed anything volleyball-related.

You didn't miss anything during that whole...

I didn't miss a thing. My kids, I think seeing me go through that journey, it made us closer because it definitely makes me more grateful for every opportunity I have. It gives me a platform to talk to them about just gratitude and just being grateful for just the opportunity. With all this Covid-19 mess... They miss going to school. I think when things are snatched... Things almost got all the way snatched from me. I almost lost my life. You become more grateful for the things that you do have. You can actually express that to a lot of people. That's been part of my mantra now.

I got to coach the Under Armor [high school all-star] game this past December in Orlando. I was telling all those athletes it was incredible to work with all those Under Armor kids. Before I left them I said, "I want you to wake up every day and think of three things that you're very grateful for and it will change your life". It will. It's changed my life drastically. I think that part has softened my heart. It's made me a different coach.

The funny thing when I got diagnosed, that little team that I had that Fall following my diagnosis probably couldn't of... I mean I calmed down. We talked about me calming down. I don't know if they could have taken me like I was. They needed this coach showing rather than the one maybe they had the year previous. It was neat to see it all unfold. It was just a huge blessing. I am grateful that I am going down this road, because it's just made my life. It's given me a platform. I've had so many people go, "You've helped so many people that you don't even realize you've helped". It's not me, it's God that's helping them. That's the thing. It's kind of neat to see that.

Breast cancer is prevalent, and so I think if any of my kids have to ever go through that journey, God love them. Maybe my experience of coaching them will help them get through it, and sharing my story. I had been pretty open and transparent about the whole journey. I think it's helped a lot of people.

I'll bet. You answered my follow-up questions, but I'm going to ask them anyway just in case anything else pops to mind. I really think it's worth touching on it again. I was going to ask you that, how that's changed your perspective on life and your coaching. You did talk a lot about it. Do you have anything you'd like to add on top of that?

Yeah. It slowed me down. I think sometimes in life we get in such a rush. You're not noticing people. I look around a lot more and observe just beauty, how beautiful a day is. People in need, I'm just a lot more empathetic toward them. If I see somebody on the side of the road, if I have any money in my wallet, I'm going to give it to them to help them. Way more empathetic. I smile a lot more, which people are scratching their heads because they can't figure it out. There's just a lot of peace that I feel now. Like I said, it's gratitude and slowing me down and just giving God the car keys to my life. Going, "Hey, whatever you want me to do, you let me know." The thing is... There have been several things that he's opened up my eyes to that I would have never seen before the diagnosis.

It sounds like a blessing in disguise that you've been lucky to realize. Do you take things from your experience regarding the adversity you've been through and the gratitude that you wanted to teach your players, and how?

I've had a bunch of my parents express how much they appreciate not the fact that I have cancer, but how open I am and how I talk to them. I think it's meant a lot to the parents. The kids obviously are going home and talking to their parents a lot about it. I'm here. I'm here for them. They have been outstanding. All these teams have been just... And even several players have reached out like crazy. It's just been amazing the support that I've gotten as well. Not just because I'm coaching now. It's been crazy. It's been way more blessings that have come out of this than not. I will say that. I know that sounds crazy, but it's the absolute truth.

All right. Moving onto the next phase of the interview. I know you're lucky enough to have an all female staff it sounds like. It's not that common to have women in coaching in Europe. There's very few of us. We are quite under-represented. What do you think are some of the barriers to females in coaching?

Well, I mean at the D1 level, the women's jobs are better than the men's. I think in the high school world, and in the club... Because there are a lot of young males in the club world who are coaching - starting out coaching these young females. Then you have these male AD's that are hiring men over women. There's more of them. There's less of us.

I think when women get married and they start raising or having a family, a lot of it is dependent on the husband. Whether he is going to help be able to take care of the kids. I know that a lot of coaches around here, they'll start out, then they start having a family. They have Kid #1, they're fine. Then, after Kid #2 they're done. I don't really know what you do about it. I don't know. We've got to somehow find more ways to get women to continue to coach. I think... I don't know. It's sad because I look around and there are too many males coaching a female sport. I think we need more female strong role models.

I think sometimes it's a matter of maybe women we're perceived to be physically and mentally weak a little bit. I don't know. I've scratched my head on that one and tried to figure it out. I think we definitely got to get more women in the game coaching.

I like the point about the role models. I think that it's very important that we do for that. We can't be what you can't see. If we don't have more females coaching, then there probably won't be more females coaching.

Right.

Are there any challenges that you've faced that you would say are unique to women or to female coaches?

Early on, I had a principal who was as not as supportive early on as the ones that I have now. It was a situation many times where we would struggle to get gym time. As we started getting successful and I started having some better relationship with the principal... It's all about respect. Not just respect with him, but respect with all of the coaches of each other. We definitely have that. My situation is not the norm necessarily. I know a lot of my friends struggle with football coaches, and if it rains they come in, take the gym over for their practices. I think it's better than it was, though. Early on, it was still a little bit of... Before Title IX just lagging a little bit.

If there was one misunderstanding or stereotype of women coaches that you would want to clear up or argue against, what would it be? Might be more than one, if you have a few.

Well, sometimes I said physically and mentally weak. Sometimes I think people think... Certain people think we are. But that's not the truth. It's far from the truth. I think we're a little bit more sensitive though. I don't know. That's one I think I was going to email you and just say, I really don't have much answer for that one. I'm trying to think. Not really. I mean, not off the top of my head.

I think you're right about the physically and mentally weak, and a little more sensitive. Yes, we are.

... Which is a good thing.

It is.

I think one of the things that somebody said to me one time, and it just kind of... It wasn't made in my head. It was about three or four years ago. One of my players who was playing club, and he was coaching her. It was top two schools. One was coached by a female and one was coached by a male. He said, "She needs to go play for a male." I thought, "Wait, what do you mean by that?" It was just kind of bizarre. I don't know. I should of asked him then what he meant by it and maybe I could answer your question a little bit better.

I guess it goes back to that point that you were saying before about the AD's being male and hiring male coaches because of what they believed to be what is necessary for a player.

Right. I think some of it too is the fear that they will start raising a household and then kind of go by the way side. Like I said, that's what happens a lot from what I see.

I have a good friend of mine, who's got two kids and she's coaching a D1 school and doing a great job. Her husband is the key. He helps out a lot.

It's a very tough job without a lot of support around.

Okay, I've got two more questions to finish up. A reading list. Do you have any books that you read or you recommend?

I'm a big Jon Gordon fan. *The Energy Bus* is one of my favorites. The one about *No Complaining Rules*. That's one of the things too. When I got diagnosed, I read that book. I did not realize how much negativity was in my life at that point. I've stepped back and I was just up at school. We can get in those rings at a school of negativity. It can really bring you down, change your attitude, and hate your job. It got me away from that

Now, I talk to people. Don't go there because you just see people all of a sudden go from loving their job to hating their job because of the people that they're hanging around, and just energy suckers, and things like that.

Chop Wood Carry Water is another one of my favorites.

That's a great book. I love that.

Yeah, that's a great book. Anyway, those are three right there. They're three of my favorites.

Do you get players to read these at all?

I do. *The Energy Bus* was one I think we read it about three or four years ago. This past year, my captain she got them to read the *No Complaining Rules* book. That was kind of neat that she took it upon herself. I mean, I didn't even have a chance to do it. She did it. That was fine with me. I think it was actually even better, and they all read it. It was phenomenal. They would have team meetings, bible studies. I mean, these two captains did a really good job of leading our team. Like I said, reading those books. They did that. Like I said, she gave it to them in the last spring.

All right. Last question. Do you have any advice for coaches just start-ing their career?

I would say, just get a mentor. Get somebody that you can talk to. Like I said, hire people that are not like you. Hire somebody that's going to bring out the best in you, and you in them. Soak up as much information as you possibly can. Know who you are. Stick with that and just tweak from there. Just have fun, and let your kids have fun. Because at the end of the day, if they're not having fun, and you're not having fun, it's just not worth it.

Winning is phenomenal, but at the end of the day we want to have fun and enjoy it and enjoy life. There you go.

Chapter Five

Saskia Van Hintum

At the time of this interview Dutch coach Saskia van Hintum was the head coach of the Swiss women's national team, though she has since left that position. She's had a long career, both as a player and a coach. This includes going to the Olympics three times – once as an indoor player, once as a beach coach, and once as an indoor coach. She's coached successfully at the club and national team level in various countries, so has a wealth of experience. After leaving the Swiss program she returned to the beach game with the national team of her native Netherlands. In this interview she talks about her experiences, coaching beach volleyball, being a high level player, and how they influenced her as a coach.

* * *

Could you start by telling us about your history and experience in volleyball? How did you get here and a little bit about your journey?

Oh well, I started when I was eight years old. So it's a long, long time ago. I'm from a soccer family. My dad was a soccer trainer and coach, so I played a lot of soccer as a little girl. It was kind of just a Wednesday afternoon from the local club, from the volleyball club, to yeah, get to know the volleyball sport. I went there and had some fun and then you could choose if you want to start playing volleyball or not. But they came up to me, so I didn't have to make the decision. They saw something and I was like, "Okay, I like it." So I started joining at eight and it went really, really quick.

I played one year with the boys. They made an exception. At the time, I think I was 11. So that saved my career, to say so. At that moment, I was already a little bit ahead with my skills. Practicing with boys at that age helped me a lot. When I was 12 I went with the seniors, and at 15 I played already in the highest league. Then 17 years in the highest league in Holland, Belgium, Germany, Italy.

At 32 I stopped playing and right away started coaching. I had the opportunity to coach the highest league women's team in Holland. I had coached already before that, though. I coached the youth and junior teams when I was playing, so I combined it. When I was playing, as a 15 year old, I started coaching 12-year-old girls.

I think I have the genes from my dad. My dad was, like I said, he was a soccer coach and trainer. I already felt early that I can share something and I want to share something, and probably yeah, join my passion with other girls and players and it's continued until now. So it's a long, long time.

Could you chat a little bit more about the places you've been coaching and sort of that journey since you've started coaching?

My first coaching was with the youth team. I started in 2000 - I was still playing – as assistant coach for the national youth team girls. After one year, I became the head coach, and then they went up with the juniors. In 2003 we had the World Champs in Thailand with the juniors. Then I got the opportunity to coach in the highest league here in Holland. I was still thinking maybe to continue playing, but I played in Belgium at that moment. There wasn't really an idea of what's going to happen with the coach there and I was like, "Okay." I had the opportunity to go full-time coaching right away and good contract in Holland. So I started that year in Amstelveen with a lot of Australian girls with this project. It was really fun.

I had a contract for two years. I went only one year, because they had another idea than I had and it was like, "Okay. I'm flexible, but if they're going to tell me how I have to do my job, that's not really the way. I want to be authentic and they can tell me, but I maybe can do better." But yeah, I want to stay close to myself and do what I think is best for the players. So then I stepped... It wasn't really step back, but I went to the second highest league in Holland for three years. I worked with a lot of younger girls. After that I stepped up again in the highest league in Holland. I was there for three years with Sliedrecht.

I have to think where I went then. My last year at Sliedrecht I combined with the beach volleyball teams – the women and the talent program. Before that, I was already coaching the beach program from 2006 and the youth development part. Yeah, so in 2009 – Summer 2009 – I stepped up to only full-time beach volleyball towards the Olympics in London with the two women's teams and two talent program teams. Then after those three years, in 2012, I went back to the indoor part, becoming a youth national girls trainer. I was there with the talent program in Papendal. They still run it. So I did this until 2016. In 2015, I became assistant coach with Giovanni [Guidetti, featured in the first Wizards book] with the women's national team. In 2016 I went to Aachen [German 1.Bundesliga]. I was there the full four years. Between for two years I was the assistant coach for Germany. So right now I'm having my new challenge in Switzerland. That's a quick review of what I did.

I have a couple of questions from that, actually. So you were a pretty high level player, you didn't mention, but an Olympian. How do you think that's influenced your coaching, if anything? What character trait has carried over, that's helped you?

I have some talents, but I really also had to work hard to get what I achieved. So the mental part helped me a lot to just get through some highs and lows which I had like a player. Especially with the national team. That's always tough, because you're chosen for a tournament and you think you're with the tournament and then one day before... I had one coach that said one day before to me "Ciao." The reason why, I still don't know until now, sort of. But at that moment, I had one goal, "I want to go to the Olympics", because that's the highest sport you can reach. By hard-working and just, "One goal. Win the Olympics and then I can go through what I want to," I reached this. Then that was when it was like, "Okay, I don't care how I get there. Maybe I only can collect goals or just carry the luggage, I really don't care." For the rest of the time, I played European Championships, World Championships. There was only one thing that I didn't achieve.

I learned a lot from this period, because I had good coaches, I had good trainers, I had good trainers and not so good coaches. All this I took with me in my coaching career and training career like, "Okay, of course everyone makes mistakes, also me." I am making mistakes still. Everyone makes mistakes. But I learned how I don't want to treat my players like I've been treated sometimes before and that was really... Yeah, that's my extra what I have as a coach now. I had this experience. Good ways and bad ways. To be an Olympian, I went there now three times – once as a player and two times like a coach. One time as a beach coach and one time indoor coach.

It's an incredible experience. You look around, not as a player, as a coach a little bit more than as player. As a player I was really more focused and as coach, I looked around a little bit more and could enjoy it a little bit more in a different way. It's really inspiring to walk around and see all the sports and see every athlete or coach, getting on the maximum level of experience and results. Even results, maybe not that, but what people expect. But yeah. Yeah, incredible journey until now.

So managing that transition from player to coaching, you took a lot of your influences from your past coaches, whether it be good or bad. We don't see a lot of high level players turn into great coaches, so I wanted to ask a little bit more about that transition and that management.

I took a lot of my experience, like I said before, from playing, but I can really remember parts of playing in Italy. Where we were far behind in the set and we won. The first set was in the playoff final. I was like, "Okay." I turned the game around again and I didn't start the second set. I can imagine, as some coach, I do the same sometimes. You want to try and maybe give the other players still the confidence, but that second set it didn't work.

So I was like, "Okay." Again, I'm ready for it, I turned the first set. So, "Give me a chance, give me a chance." But I didn't get any chance at all, the rest of the match and we lost the match. I was like, "Okay, this is something I have to take with me and learn from it" and I don't say that I'm not doing this at all as a coach now, because sometimes it's just a split second decision which you make with substitution or not. But it's just a small example.

I had some moments also with the national team that my coach said, "Okay, you get a chance you can show in a tournament" and this and that. I showed it and at the end, he was still doubting me. I was like, "Okay, you ask me, you were telling me something. I show what you want me to show you, but you're still doubting, so then be honest. I'm really honest. Be honest to me, then tell me, 'I'm looking for something different.'" I mean that's what I look for and that's what I'm doing with my players. I'm honest, I will tell them. They can ask me and I will tell them. I never will send them away and I will always tell them when I make a mistake and I have to do it different after a game. They come to me and I say, "Why this and this?" They never have to come and whine. They're not coming to whine, which is... I give them the opportunity to ask the question, "Why?" Or maybe I was like, "Yeah okay, you're right." Ask now which I'm thinking back and I have to change.

I think that's good to have a good connection with players. Not sending them away, it's not only my crew. Yeah, it's you have to do it together. That's sometimes what I missed as a player. Of course, you can talk with the coach. But in that time, it was like, "Okay, I'm the coach and that's how it is" and I mean we had the little chit chats with the coach, but in the end I didn't always feel that respected. I had to work hard, so that you could wake me up at 6:00 in the morning and put me in the gym the whole day and I would work my ass off. I did and I showed that I had some possibilities to play in the highest level. I did it my way and I'm really proud how I did it. So yeah, that made me bigger, greater as a player, but I think I have a lot of luggage in my backpack as a coach now also to use.

So if I could summarize - you can correct me if I'm wrong - but the empathy that you have from being a player and just understanding how the players are feeling in certain situations, that's something that you find has helped you in your transition to coaching.

Yeah, like I said, I mean I'm also still making mistakes. I mean after matches, I think, "Oh dammit, I had to do a substitution." But you cannot change it. As a coach, I think you can say... My coach at that time in Italy, I think he could have said after match, "Okay, sorry. I had the possibility I had to put you in back again." Maybe it didn't work, but at least offer. It's not a big deal to say, "Sorry, I made a mistake." Yeah, I don't know. maybe it's us women, where maybe it's easier for us to say. I don't know, Lauren. But I think for men, some kind of men, it's difficult. But I think yeah, there are coaches that can do it the same way. I think it's important.

I 100% agree and I think it's an important skill that players appreciate. So it's good to hear that that's something you took from your playing career.

All right, you mentioned before that they told you how to do the job and you wanted to be authentic in your coaching. Could you maybe give us a little bit of an example from that time?

Yeah, it was interesting. They had a president and he was the president/owner of the club. I came in and he respected me as a player, because I had played then a lot, of course, in Holland. I had a young team in this project with some Australian players. I had some young players from my junior team and a whole new team. It takes time, it takes time.

So the practicing went well. Okay, we didn't win that many matches. Then suddenly came the club boss – the club was called IMVA – and when he came I had a meeting with him. He said "You're not playing the IMVA way." I was like, "Sorry? What's the IMVA way? You hired me to be the coach. I'm doing my job. I mean girls are progressing, practicing good. Okay, we're not winning, but it's still developing and it's about the players."

So I was like, "Okay. I have my way to coach, I have my way to practice. It's working well. It's not that it sucks." But yeah, I had a two year contract and at the end of the first year I said, "Okay, if you want me to do it only the way you think you want to do it, then it's not me." I mean I didn't ask them how they want me to do it, because I was not like, "Okay, there's no one way."

That confused me a little bit, because I enjoyed what I did. I mean it was okay. I had a good contract with him, but just tell someone, "This is the way we have to do it." They have to tell me before I signed the contract. You go somewhere and they tell me, "If you come here and you want to work with us, then you have to do it this way." Then I can decide, "Okay, I can do it that way and put something from me in it." But in the end that's what I also don't like, when people or also players come to me after the season and tell me, "Yeah that happened before for six months," or "That happened and why did it?" I was like, "Yeah, you have to tell me." I cannot change that anymore.

So yeah, I mean I choose for myself at that moment. I didn't choose for the money. I had a really good contract for Holland and I was like, "No, this is not me. It's not." So I said, "Okay, ciao. Look for someone else." I learned a lot from it, but choosing for myself, saying for myself [not to] be dependent on them, or the money, that they give me. So it was not an important part. I want to coach like I want to coach. I want to be me.

How has that influenced future jobs that you've taken? Have you tried to find out in advance what they want you to do?

No, not really, it wasn't necessary. The next club where I went was to Red-mond. It's in the west part of Holland, so it's a different culture. I'm from the south part. I mean, Holland is small, but we still have the differences. They wanted me really badly and we had a good conversation and I had the way I wanted to work and they were really open for it. The first year was really interesting, because I had the World Champs and I came in only... I think I had one week before the competition started, so it was also very interesting. I had kind of an assistant who did my preparation, and I came in and I had the first practice and I was like, "What the heck? What did they do all those weeks?" But I fixed it and we had a good season.

Like I said, every time, the next step, I did this three years and I could step up to see the next spot again. I had the freedom to do what I wanted to do. I mean it's not that they told me what I had to do. I always want to cooperate with the club and show my interest, not only in the first team, but also in the youth. So I did something with the youth programs, and the beach volleyball was the same.

So my first experience was not the worst one, but the one where I had to, "Okay, if this is going to happen to again", then probably I would ask them or tell them what I think. So 'til now if I come somewhere, of course I tell them how I want to work and goal for it. It's not only my vision. It's my way. That doesn't mean that someone else can't add something to it. Like I said, I want to work together with people and not let people say, "Okay, I'm the boss and this is it." Maybe I was lucky with the next steps I made, but until now that has worked out very well.

Could you tell us about some coaching influences, whether it be initial or ongoing. I know you mentioned your father was a coach, so maybe he's one of them. But, after that?

I learned as a player a lot from the coaches who had coached me. I look at a lot of matches [in the] Italian League and see what's possible, and I always put the volume up when the camera is going in the timeouts. Just to listen to what coaches say, and sometimes try to learn, and sometimes I'm like, "Hmm. Okay, that's easy, on that level, also."

But I don't know really. I think I picked from everyone maybe a little bit. I worked with Giovanni Guidetti. He is, I think, one of the best in what he's doing. He's really authentic and he did some stuff I already did a little bit, so it was nice to see. But I never copied someone. I don't want to be a copy of someone. I want to learn from people. I learned from Giovanni. I worked with Felix [Koslowski] with the German national team. We learned from each other. I have an open-mind to watching coaches.

Also, from other sports. It's not only volleyball. I worked four years in Papendal with the talent programs and I had a really good contact with, for example, the wheelchair basketball coaches. It's interesting to see how they work and it's amazing. One of my best friends, she was one of the handball coaches. So it's just, get information, listen to each other. Get in conversations with people and learn how to take out of it what you can use. I read a lot of articles from different kinds of stuff. I take from everyone, everywhere a little bit and use what I can use.

Maybe there's one of the greatest coaches. He has a certain kind of way of working or coaching. It has to suit me. If it's not suiting me, then I'm not going to coach [his way]. He's the best in what he's doing, but that's his way. With the reading part, it's also helping me a lot to still get some small information and technical, tactical, mentally, with nutrition, physiology, with everything. So I think I take a lot out of those things also.

How has your coaching philosophy changed over time?

It's not only coaching, but also the training part. Ten years ago, maybe a little bit longer, I started training and coaching, telling my players what we're going to do, how they have to do it, and every single detail. Now I tell them what we're going to do in practice, I tell them which exercises we're going to do and just let them figure out how they can do it. Make a mistake. Let them think about it themselves, instead of telling them what to do or what to expect. Just let them go and let them start with the exercise.

That's really changed a lot. I mean, that's a big difference. What's really fun is... I think it starts with the part of the culture. In general, I think it's more individual than in my time when we were playing. We were more together. We didn't have that many distractions. So for example, I had my school and I had my volleyball. Now there are different kinds of distractions, of course with social media, with the phone, with everything around you. The focus is different. They don't have to communicate, or think themselves that much anymore, as we had to do in our time, I think. So yeah, I want to get them to do this a different way now.

Like I said, there was a pretty fixed span of time, and I was flexible, but I became more flexible over the years. I can remember my first year at Papendal, the talent program, I was really still like this. The players came in and they were like still five minutes before, they were not ready and as a player I was really focused. I didn't drink. No coffee. Not too much distractions and I came in and I was like "What the heck? What are they doing?" But that's how it is today and yeah, I grow with this culture.

I know a lot of trainers and coaches in Holland... I call it old school. They still work old school.

Also, the technical part. I think a lot of talents are missed out, because your play changed a lot. Some of our coaches and trainers in Holland, they still are doing it how it was before. I'm looking at different techniques at the international level. Learn from the best and get [what you can] out of that area.

So you gave the example of players. You'd let them start the exercise and figure it out and ask questions and stuff like that. What made you realize that that was a better way to do things for you?

Because the play changed. It's like here at home. You would try to get rid of some stuff you really had a long time. I began with DVD when I was playing and then the play changed. It became quicker. So the brain has to react and make these quicker decisions. I mean when we were playing... Okay, we played quick in that time, because that time the ball was coming over and you had time, but that changed also. So my players also have to be able to think quicker and on their own ,and be independent from me. They have to be themselves.

I mean I always say, "I can help you until a certain time, a certain moment. But the last part, you always have to do yourself." I want them to learn this and to make a decision. Maybe you make a bad decision. You have to make bad decisions, because you don't know. If you don't make a decision at all, you don't know if it was a good one, or it was not a good one.

And like I said, just the culture, that changed. People how they... We could do one hour the same drill in our practice. Nowadays, I don't give them one hour the same drill. They get bored. We could do just repetitions. Now they want to have a score, they want to have a challenge. That changed.

So I had to go with this, but it came step by step and I figured it out. I saw it. They didn't say,"We don't like it, what you do", but yeah, sometimes my place is like, "Okay, we do it this way, or maybe you can go with the counting, or just like yeah, yeah, just do it." That was like, "I know, I'm so fixed. You do it only this way." Yeah, it's challenging. It's challenging myself also with making drills, sitting down, thinking about different countings and different challenges they have to do.

That's also for me, that keeps me going. I mean otherwise, I would have just sat down and still do the same. No, I would have been quitting. Yeah, so just like I said, the players and the play that's involved. Ask it from me and yeah, I went with it. I had to go with it, because otherwise I cannot step up like a coach and a trainer and I would still be on the same level for 10 years, I think.

I'm going to ask you a bit more specifically about Aachen. You were pretty successful there, and as far as I understand, on quite a lower budget than the top teams in Germany. What were the keys that you focused on when you took the job to help turn this around?

Yeah, in one way I was lucky. When I came there, there was nothing. I mean the organization was still there. All the players left because they had some financial issues at the moment. So it wasn't clear if they would continue or not. But I said, "Okay." I stepped in. I still had one goal as a coach to coach abroad, and I had this opportunity in Aachen, so I said, "Okay, I'm going to do it."

There was nothing – no players anymore, no coach, no assistant. I could build it from the bottom up. Also, in the organization, they did some good things, but I reached out on some things where I said, "Okay, but I think still we can improve with some stuff." I looked for some players and started working a lot also with individuals, sort of to develop younger players – lower budget. So we get in younger players who wanted to make their first step abroad, but was closer to home. There was the advantage of Aachen. Also, a little bit older players who also wanted to get a chance to play abroad that may be not that far away, but still have a chance to get this experience.

We were working with a lot of individuals, not putting the result in the first place, in the beginning. Which they called it a project, because we get in there some younger players and develop them. Then we know, "Okay after one, two, maybe three years they will leave." If they became a better player, then I did my job good.

So I told also Aachen, the advantage is that they know me, they probably will come to Aachen, because they know who I am and how I work. The disadvantage is, "Okay, they will leave." Because, they become better players, they will leave to better teams, but they're the top teams. They said, "Okay, if you want to work in this project we will start" and yeah, people liked it.

I mean the fans didn't like it a lot in the beginning, because they are used to, "Okay, but this player, this team. She was good and now she's leaving, after maybe one year or two years." I was like, "She became a better player. She will get her chance in one of the top teams and we have to accept this."

So yeah, it was a new challenge, a new project for me, from something different, something new. Something, like I said, from zero. It was perfect for me and I liked it.

It was not the first time. I had a kind of same experience when I was working in Sliedrecht. The team was almost going down to the second league and I didn't have that many players. I had to get players out of the third and fourth league, let them grow. Yeah, so I really like to get a challenge and I like to work in the national team with players who are already almost there. But you never will be there, because you're always learning during your career until the end, I think.

But yeah, like I said, the development of players first and yeah, get the team spirit out of it. A little bit closer to me just to work hard, work your ass off and get the most out of it. And with different kinds of talents. So it's not only the best players who are coming, which it's also players where I think, "I see this and this and I can make them a better volleyball player," or the mental part." Helping them to be a better person also, not only a better volleyball player.

So that sort of culture you changed to be a spot where players could come and develop and be a better player and then move on? Because I mean you had to whether you wanted to or not. But you had some good results as well on the end of this work.

Yeah, I mean in my first year I had 11 players and eight players stayed. So that was my luck, I think in one way. But I think that was good, so we could continue the work which I started, so the players knew how I was working.

Then in the end we were at a good position and we won the bronze medal. Then the third year, we kicked Dresden – one of the top teams – out of the quarter finals. So we played the semi-finals again and we won a bronze medal again – with a whole new team, by the way. But I mean the culture was there. The organization knew what to expect from me. The fans knew how we were working and the players who stayed know how I'm working.

So it was always good to have a few players who were there, who stayed and yeah, just could pass on my philosophy on what I wanted to do and what I expect.

I'm always honest directly in the beginning of the season what I expect, what they can expect from me. And we start working and during the season, with the ups and downs, we will manage a lot of things. Like I said before, the cooperation is for me really, really important. I mean the player... I always say, "Please come to me, tell me." I mean, I'm also one of them. I mean, "Come ask me after practice" and sometimes they say, "Okay, this we didn't like that much," or, "That was good."

I'm still learning every day. That's the culture I want to have with the people I work with, so not that I'm, "Okay, you're the boss now." I mean, I always say, "We're equal." For me, my staff is equal, my players are equal. In the end, I make the decision, so I step up a little bit. In the end, I'm responsible for what we're doing, but we have to do it together, I cannot do it alone.

You've mentioned a little bit about the culture and the club. What about the team culture? What's important for you and how do you build it?

Like I said, in the beginning I always tell them that, "I'm going to be honest with you, so I also want that you're going to be honest with me." Giving the players and my staff the possibility to talk to me and also tell me when I'm doing things not the best way maybe you should do. That's important for me. Yeah, work hard and have fun in what you do. I mean like I said, for me, I've already been a long time now with full-time player, full-time coach, I still don't see it as my job. I mean I see it as my hobby.

I always say, "If I'm really going to see it as my job, then I'm going to miss my passion, my motivation, because then I have to do what I'm doing, rather than wanting to do what I'm doing." That's also what I want to do with my players, with the team. They have to want to come into practice.

Of course, sometimes they come into practice like, "We're tired." I mean like everyone. We also sometimes think, "Oh no, not today." "Okay, you come in the gym and it's this. You do your job and then you go." Sometimes you have a team where you think you need team-building. I mean you have to do something special. Some exercises, some drills in the gym, can be also be enough to get the team bonded and that they stick together.

The communication part for me is really one main thing. I cannot work without communication. I will get crazy. Also, when I go to players, or to my coach and someone runs away, not answering, I'm like, "Come on, give me an answer". I ask questions. I want them to respond and try to get out what I think I need to get out of them. Even if it's a player, but also one of my staff members. It's important.

Jumping on the team-building stuff. Do you believe in team-building? Are there any specific team-building activities you do?

I did different kinds of things. I did one when I was working with Sliedrecht, I did it always. Just the last weekend before the competition started. So there were a lot of coaches they started the team-building in the beginning of the preparation. I did it at the end of my preparation. Just do something different. We didn't play volleyball. Yeah, do some cooperation stuff. Get also some other people in, so that I can watch who is going to take responsibility, who is going to take initiative, who is going to step back.

Most of the time, you already saw this before, but it's always good to see it in a different way and just have something fun in a different way. Just sit together and talk about goals, what they want to achieve. It has to be a goal from the team. It's not going to be my goal. I mean let this be our goal, but at the end, the team has to do it.

So that's how I did it at that time. Sometimes I wasn't there in some preparation parts when I was in Aachen, because I was in Rio, or I was in Japan for the World Champs. But in Aachen it was pretty easy sometimes, because they came from everywhere. They were somewhere alone there in Aachen, so they bonded together on their own. It was a different way.

Then, of course, if I saw something like I thought, "Hmm, we need to do more communication, or cooperation." I did have some drills to do in the gym and that they have to trust each other. Or we did once with Aachen on the way back [from a road trip]. We had a tournament in Paris and on the way back on Sunday in Belgium somewhere to get some juice. What's needed, I do. It's not like that's fixed in my program.

I mean, going out for dinner, having a beer together. This is also team-building.

Yeah, it's important.

Like I said, they need it, they need this. We could do this earlier, for a long, long time ago. But they need this. I also always invite them to have a beer with me. Not always that they do it, but I'm happy that some players just do this – come with me and drink a beer with me. So that's okay.

You mentioned you set goals with the team and it's the team's choice about what they want to achieve. Do you do that every year, as a similar process?

No, no. It changed also. I have in my mind what I want to achieve. Until now, almost every time the team had the same view, I think because we work together and then in the end, they know how we can work and what we can achieve. I like to go with more steps.

So for example, if you play a competition you say first you want to get that position in a competition for playing play-offs. You get a good position to see which team we will meet. Then we can say, "Okay, what's going to be our next step?" I did this with the youth and junior teams which I worked with also. So, "Okay, we have a pool. We have a pool and we want to reach..." Of course, at the end, you want to get at the podium. I mean you want to go to the highest you can get.

But first, you have to get out of the pool and get better and also the best results and positions. So it changed a little. It's what suits the culture and what suits the players and I will work with that. I cannot copy what I did in Aachen, or what I did with Sliedrecht, or what I did with the juniors. Yeah, like I said, I just see what's needed and I'm going to adjust, and it can be different ways get bonded as a team, or get a team all together.

What about the leadership and captain selection? How do you select captains and what are their responsibilities?

Yeah, that's always a good thing with captain selection. Sometimes it was obvious. If you have a lot of young players, you don't have that many experienced players, then it's good to have a little bit more experienced players to get this responsibility. That doesn't mean that a younger player cannot have this responsibility. But a younger player has to feel that she is ready for it.

I had last season an example, I asked one of my younger players and she was like, "Hmm, I don't think I'm ready for it." After, during the season, she was like, "I was ready for it." But she didn't know. It's always a little difficult, because maybe there are older players in the team and she was like "Maybe not." But in the end, she was more ready than she expected herself. I saw it, I knew it, that she could do it.

But sometimes I just make a player a captain for her development, just to get more out of herself in a different way. To take on more responsibility. Sometimes it works. It worked one year in Aachen good, one year it didn't work the way I thought it would work. I mean it didn't damage the team at all, but that's happened.

So, it's different ways sometimes. One time, I asked players, I said, "Who do you think would be a good captain?" Yeah, it depends a little bit from the group also. How the group fits together and if people are ready for it. You just get people personal... Like I said, sometimes they are ready. It's the most obvious for everyone to get a captain, but not always for me. I mean that's the player who always will take on responsibility, or talk a lot, or whatever. Sometimes it's good to give a player responsibility, to learn from this and get a better player this way.

And I talk, not a lot. I talk a lot with all my players, but if you make different decisions, or maybe make a schedule change, or time change, then yeah. I talk with the captain. I always have two. So I have a captain to do the toss, because I want to have a captain that she has someone which she can talk also, to have a little bit of conversation and she's not standing alone. Not that she cannot handle me alone, but it's always good to have. It's soothing also. You have one captain and the other one you see she's already organizing a lot of stuff, taking initiative with some things. So it doesn't have to be always the captain who is the most important player for me. I mean someone has to be captain, it's not that she has more to say than someone from 18 years.

So you choose the captain yourself?

Yeah most of the time I did. Like I said, one year I asked the other players, "Who do you think is the best option?" I think I asked one time in Sliedrecht. I did it different ways, and I think that most of the time, almost every time, the one who I had in my mind, yeah they picked also. So yeah, I did it differently. Like I said, again, it depends on the group.

Shifting topic a little, in discussing developing team concepts or systems, do you have set ideas that you work with in each phase of player – whether it be a side out or a break point [service], for example? Or are you adapting?

I mean I had some technical concepts, but I think it's important how we can work with it. I had good results. And the way we play, I like to play a little bit quicker, if possible. If it's possible and if you have the play for it, or be more flexible. Because I was a setter, I coach my setters also.

But I don't like to tell them what they have to play. I want them to have an idea, so we make a plan. If they make a plan and it's really, really not what

I think we should do, I'm going to help them and I'm going to give them advice. Sometimes of course, I will say, "In this situation, for now, we're going to run this and this." I'm not telling them what they have to play in the moment, but normally if I say a certain kind of run, I hope they know who they have to set in the moment, in an important situation.

I mean sometimes you can have a really fixed... You have to give them more help in what we need to play. But I want them to learn themselves what we can play and what's better not to be played – depending on our technical ability, in receiving, in attacking. What can my setters play? Are they are able to run a quick game? I mean I can't tell them, "We're going to run a quick game", if my setter can only set a little bit more up and down. Then, of course I will definitely work on this part. But in the end, if she's not comfortable with it, then I have to adjust a little bit. Most of the time, they figure it out in the way we play.

I have my ideas and it's not fixed. Like I said, I'm flexible. If there's another player coming in and she can run more combinations and she wants to and the team is able to handle this, then we can do it. I like to see some good volleyball, so that's to me important. I also want to enjoy the game when I'm standing on the sidelines watching. So yeah, like I said, my ideas are coming from the individual skills from the players, and of course, the impact on the team, what they're able to achieve.

How do you manage different parts of the season? If we're talking about preseason through to finals, what a week of training will look like, or how is it different?

In the preparation, during the season, I still do a lot of individual stuff, so I keep developing my players to get them a better player in different kinds of ways. It's not only in the beginning. I continue with this part.

Yeah, in the preparation, some different kind of stuff, like letting them learn to know each other a little more as individuals. So building up. But the general thing is there's not a big, big difference in the way I practice during the season, or during playoffs. We have of course, at the end, during the season sometimes, if you play European Cup or [domestic] Cup, or the playoffs, then you have to adjust your time a little bit, and intensity.

But I'd rather practice intense and a little bit shorter, than longer like we did. I practiced four hours when we were with the national team. So two hours in the morning, four hours in the afternoon, we practice six hours a day. It's a little bit different nowadays. There's not, like I said, a really big difference.

What about coaching in training or preparation, versus match coaching. What do you think is more important and why?

I want to coach them most of the part during my training, so they know what they can do, what they still have to learn to do in the game. So they take it with them in the matches. In the matches I just want to still help them a little bit, sometimes a little bit technical, sometimes a little bit mentally. For the rest, I just keep them going.

I always say the best way is if I take a timeout and I don't have to say anything. Those are the best timeouts, because then they're doing a good job. But it starts at the training, at the practices. Not only before. It starts already before the training for me and after training. It's not, "Come in, practice, go home." It's everything around it. It's about connection, every moment with everyone. It's not only with your players who play more and other players who play less.

It's for me, they're equal. I know they don't feel always equal, because one is playing more than the other one. So of course, there is always an issue in every team. But that's for me, not a difference. I tell them also, I mean, "You are equal. So you can come to me as much as the other players can do."

With the coaching part, like I said, I like trainings. But I think maybe also because of my beach period, the coaching part I like the most, because there you get more out of it, of course. I always say everyone can run a practice. I mean everyone can find a drill and tell a drill. But if you cannot get [something] out of it, on an individual level, this is coaching. Get the connection with the player and make her better. Yeah then you can be the best trainer in the world, but if the coaching part is missing, it's going to be difficult, I think. So yeah. Like I said, I like the individual connection a lot and I think it's important.

We'll jump to beach quickly then. You've coached both beach and indoor on a pretty high level. Do you think there's transfer between the two? Did coaching beach have any influence on your indoor coaching?

It's really funny, because when I was playing indoor and we were talking about playing beach, all the coaches were like, "No, you're not allowed to go play beach. It's so bad for you if you go in the sand." I was like, "Okay. Don't worry." I mean I played in the national team, but the players who didn't play and had the Summer off, I was like, "Let them go in the sand. I mean it's really good."

I'm happy this changed, but when I came in the sand... It was like my team, when I coached at Sliedrecht, my players already went in the sand in the Summer. So I didn't have to give them a summer program, because they played the whole Summer beach. It was perfect. You keep in shape and for the individual skills.

In coaching the beach, the individual coaching part is important. The individual, but also the team part. I mean, okay, there is only two of them, but I had one tournament where it was going well, then one match they lose and first one the girls came to me and [frustrated noise]. They had a little bit of a fight. Then later the other one came. So this was also kind of a team-building, just the two of them, because they are more depending on each other than in a club team. I managed it. I spoke with both and they fixed it and they won the tournament. They [chuckles] became European Champions U23.

There I find the intensity working with the individual player a lot also and it helps me to recognize the individual player, when she feeling maybe not that well, or doing not that well. Not only the individual part. It's not only the volleyball part, because with beach volleyball you're traveling around a lot. Maybe with two, maybe with four. Sometimes you're alone, because you don't want to have time together always, because you're always doing together every time, everything. So it's also leave them alone.

You're not allowed to coach with beach volleyball. Perfect! Give them their own responsibility. I like that, really, really a lot. So there I had to do my coaching during the training and let it go and enjoy the game, during the game they played. Just sit down and analyze and talk with them after about what they have to do better. Then in two hours, maybe an hour and a half, they have to play the next game. So it just feels like, "Make the next step, quick. Don't stick with it, step up. You don't have time to think about what went wrong maybe, but yeah, fix it. Think about what we can do better." I think that made me also even more flexible.

Also, probably in indoor now, like I said, I came from a pretty fixed thing, what I did before. So, being more independent. Also for players, I give my players also a lot of responsibility, as a team. Of course, I have my rules – what I like to see. But if the team says, "Yeah, but if we do it this way, it suits us better." "Okay, just do it."

It's more fun sometimes. People ask me, "What did you like more, the beach or indoor?" It's so different, you cannot compare. It's so different. It's a different way of living, different style. Okay, you play both. It's volleyball, but it's different and it's good that players can do both a little bit. They can learn a lot out of it. I always say, if a player would say, "I'm maybe not involved with a national team, or I want my club team, I want to go play beach in the summer." Yeah, I always say, "Yeah, go for it." So yeah.

Okay. Switching topics a little bit, I would like to talk about selecting staff, your assistant coaches and coaches. How do you do that? What's important to you and what are their roles in the team?

Until now, I worked with pretty young and little bit less experienced assistant coaches, because I like to give my experience as a trainer and a coach to trainers and coaches. For me, it's important that we have good communication. It's huge. One time I had a woman that I didn't work all that well, only half a season.

But yeah, I give them a responsibility. They need to do it. It's a little bit different if it's in the national team, or a club team, sometimes. For me, the assistant is responsible to get all the information before the matches, from out of the Data Volley. I will do the preparation. We do the video preparation together. During the matches, sometimes I say, "You look at the opponent, or the defense, or the attacking system and I will be responsible for our own team in some way." Of course, I will look on the other side of the net, but what I see of course, I will say.

It depends a little bit on which kind of skills he has. He has to get involved – do one practice, maybe more – so I always can back off a little bit and watch it from a different kind of view, so I don't always have to be in front of my team. But also kind of a different role. Good communication.

My medical staff is important. I didn't have many here in Aachen, so I gave them the responsibility to have good communication. Like I said, for me the communication part is what's important, and they have to have good coaching skills. It's important if I say, "You have to hit the ball left from the player that the ball will come on the left for the player." Of course, it can sometimes be a little bit, change up a little bit. But that's important if you want to practice individual skills. We need to be able to put the ball where we can challenge them.

I worked with players who played not always on the highest level, but some played on the highest level and some played a little bit lower level, but they have good skills.

They have to want to learn, also.

Until now that has worked out well, so.

You talked a little bit then about that you've integrated Data Volley into your program, but what other kind of technology or statistics are you using in your different roles that you've worked in?

To be honest, in the beginning, I did analyze my opponent and my own team, but I didn't work that much with it, because I was like, "If we are not able to play our own game..." I can give a lot of information... When I was working in Sliedrecht. I really had an unexperienced team,who had to learn a lot. I give them a small informations, just to recognize stuff, and step by step I could give them more information.

For myself, I didn't get that much out of it. I think I learned to get more out of it when I worked with Giovanni, with all the paperwork. He had a little booklet with everything. I learned to read this and take more out of it at the moment, to see that makes a difference. I think if you work at the highest level, the last percentages are important.

Now I work kind of the same way. I always take my little booklet and I go through different kind of numbers. I am not only relying on the numbers, because that doesn't always say everything for me. I'm watching some- times also the whole match, just to see how a team is reacting, or my team is reacting. For example, the match report after our own match. It's just numbers. I mean it doesn't say always everything.

But yeah, like I said, step by step I start joining it more and getting more out of the Data Volley stuff. I like to work with a live delay during my matches. I really do a lot with a live delay on an iPad, because I can give them a little advice on the blocking part, or the hitting skill, or whatever. And because we worked on this probably also during the week, then I can remind them, give them a little reminder. Until now, my players liked it a lot – to get some more feedback just shortly.

You get used to it. If my iPad is not working and I don't have it, then I'm like "Oh damn it. Where is my feedback?" Of course you see, but it's good to have. It's fun to work with.

You have hinted a lot at this answer, but as coaches we need to be quite knowledgeable in a lot of areas, whether it be technical, tactical, or personal. What do you think are the most important qualities for a coach?

Like I said, I think what's important for me, is the personal part. Of course, my job is to make them a better volleyball player, but if I can make them... I'm not going to *make* them. If I can *help* them to become a different person than they came in with me in the beginning of the season, in certain kind of areas where they probably didn't know they could do, or they dared to do, or dared to talk, and they leave after and I see this big change from when they came in at the beginning of the season and they leave at the end of the season, then they will take it with them the rest of their career and the rest of their life.

The volleyball moment, okay this technical thing she will hear, or he will hear also from a different coach the next year, or in a couple of years, maybe in a different way. But I think the personal way, the coaching part is for me what I'm enjoying a lot. Then the technical part... I like to develop my players and [teach] them, just on the easiest way to feel a difference. If it's in the national league, or in the highest league, or just coaching some youth players here from the local club – which I did now a few times – and they do it and you say something and they were like, "I did something different." Yeah, I enjoy this a lot.

And let them feel safe, they have to feel safe, so yeah.

Looking back, what are some mistakes you've made and things you've learned, or changes you've made from those mistakes?

Like I said, sometimes after a match, that I was waiting to make substitution – or waiting for a split second maybe to do or don't – and after the match, "Okay, I have to do this differently," or "I had to put in the player that I didn't do."

So this is one thing I always will admit to myself. Always after a match, the first thing I do is look to myself. The question I will always ask... Of course if you're winning it's easy, but if you lost the match then I'm asking the question always to myself, "What could I have done differently to help my team?" I'm not blaming my team that they didn't do things first. Of course, if they did, I will help them to remind that we had some agreements on some stuff. But yeah, so that's for me important to react on this part for myself first.

Just a couple things about your personal experience. You've worked in both national teams and clubs. Can you describe a little bit the experience working in both those areas and their differences?

I think the clubs are, for me, it's always a difference. For me it has to be an honor to play for your national team. There has been... A small example has been a period in Holland. There were players they rejected to play for the national team because they didn't get paid something. Then I get crazy. Then I was like, "Come on! There has to be an honor." I mean your club is where you're going to and normally you will get your money, and representing your country has to be an honor. That's the best way you can get out of yourself, to represent yourself to the world together, to get the European Championships, or the World Champs, or the Olympics. I mean I think that's one way.

Club teams is like yeah, it's learning new people and learning new cultures, if people go play abroad and it's a different kind of organization. National teams are supposed to be more professional organizations, but also club teams have, meanwhile, really good professional organization, in every part of the world.

So yeah, like I said, national teams that's where you're normally working for to get in. I mean, in my time, it was only 12 players. Now it can be a little bit more, but it's not for everyone to get selected for your national team. I think it doesn't have to be a main goal, but if you're able to and you can represent your country, I think it can be really an honor.

You just mentioned it there a little bit, but you're coaching different cultures, whether it be in a national team or within a club. How do you manage that and can you talk about some experiences coaching different cultures?

I think you have to respect where you are. We have different mentalities in Holland. In Germany, there's a different mentality. In Swiss, there is a different mentality. I always tried… I'm going to try to get the best out of the mentality and adjust and give them some extra that they can help to maybe get out of their culture. Most of the times, it's getting them a little bit out of their comfort zone to make a change.

In some cultures, and if it's too good for you…

We always have the classical example. Maybe there are countries that really have to work their ass off to get where they want to be, because they don't have something else. I mean maybe in Brazil, one of the younger players, they're living in the flavelas. They don't have anything and they have the opportunity to get into the national team and help their families to change their life. Where we come from, if you're not making it as a professional athlete, then you go study and find a job.

So we always have a different thing behind which we can rely on. Or we have a good system that we still can survive and we still can live in a good way. That's what we sometimes miss mentally. I mean the killing mentality, like different countries have. We have to change this. We have the opportunity to work on it. That's different.

Holland, Germany, Swiss, it's a little bit kind of the same mentality, I think, with small changes. If I would go in a different culture where we would have to survive – a real good culture in Africa, where they have to survive – I will find a different culture and work with other skills and with other personalities than I did 'til now. But I still want to make a change, one way or the other.

I like that.

Moving on, the title of this series is "The Wizard Women", so it's a series targeted at female coaches. I'm really happy to be able to help put some top female coaches into the spotlight a little bit. Related to that, the first question I have to ask is why did you want to be a part of this?

You already said it. There are not that many female coaches.

I always get this question, "Why not?" I don't know. I'm thinking about it a lot, not a lot, but more often. I mean, I can imagine the players, I always ask my national team players or other players like, "Can you imagine you're going to be a coach or a trainer?" [They're] like, "No, no, no. I'm not going to be. I don't have the patience for it." So now families, other careers, studies, other interests, issues they want to be or want to do.

I don't know. It's not that we're not able to. I mean there are not enough. Of the examples there are. They have good experience and they have good results in what they do, in different kinds of sports. It's not that there are not. But yeah, I like to show. I think I follow my heart, and if female coaches are out there and they want to follow their heart, just do it and get organized.

I don't know. Maybe you have to be lucky with your partner. I was lucky with my partner always – didn't step back but he said, "Yeah, okay. I like what you do with the career."

Yeah, it's important, but I mean we're really good enough. We're really good enough to do it and we can handle the men's world. We have just to do it and if you do it, then you will find out that you're able to.

So you mentioned that your supportive partner was very important for you to be able to continue on your coaching journey. What else has been important?

Like what do you mean? Like important for-

A support system, a mentor, to help you continue growing in your coaching journey, as a female specifically, because it is just not that common that there are females at your level.

I give a lot of clinics. I'm spreading out my experience in Holland. If coaches want to watch my trainings, or want to talk with me, I always invite them. If they have questions, I'm always open to share those things. Sometimes moms with young girls are like, "I have a question." I hope I can help them, and I would like to train trainers. If there were some women who would say, "I really want to get there," then I will be the first one to help them and lead them where they can go.

In the volleyball world, I see in different sports. It's more common now in the soccer world. I think it's more common now in the women's part. Basketball is getting a little bit more, I think. Yeah, like I said. I don't know. I really want to give them the opportunity to get in. That's one of my ideas, but if I have more time, then I will yeah, help out to coach a coach, or do different kind of stuff.

Did you have that opportunity yourself? Was that something that was given to you as a female, from other female coaches, or not?

No, not really. I mean I had one when I was still a young player, I had one female who helped me thinking about my decision to make my first step abroad. I think it's good to have someone where you can talk to and get some advice. It's not that they're going to tell you what to do, but just step up to someone and ask them, not for help, but just for some advice. At the end you're going to make the decision.

I think it's more common as a woman to step to a woman than to a man, in general. Just don't be too proud of yourself. Make this step and ask. Like I said, it's not asking for help, it's asking for advice, to help you grow.

Have there been any challenges that you've faced that are unique to female coaches? Or that's specifically to you, that you have faced that is because you are female?

I don't know what I did, or what I do, but where I went, I was accepted right away. I didn't really have the challenge. Maybe the way I work, or the way I cooperate with people, they liked a lot. They saw also where I'm able to... Like I said, I just did the things that were good to do like that way and it worked out.

It's not that I was like, "Okay, I have to do it this way." No, I did it a way and I'm honest, in the beginning. They ask me, "Why are you a good coach?" I always said, "Ask my players", because at that moment, I did what I did and it worked out. I mean in 30 years you learn a little bit more from yourself. I'm pretty lucky, I think.

Okay, not always the easiest question to answer, but are there any misunderstandings or stereotypes of female coaches that you would want to clear up, or argue against?

I don't know. For me, what I would like to see maybe a little bit more in our volleyball world, for example, Italy. Italy really isn't... I mean they have maybe a more man culture on the head level. But yeah, I think the culture's changing. The world is changing. There are more women becoming directors of big companies, or CEO's of big companies.

I think this change is going through in the company world. Why not in the sports world? So this would be an interesting situation to see what's happening there, and why is it happening there, and accept it maybe more than in the sports world. Maybe they show themselves a little bit more. I think we have to show ourselves a little bit more to step up.

Just go to not waiting. I think maybe we were waiting too much. Waiting that they come to us and ask them, "You want to be our head coach?" I mean, men are more likely to step up like, "Here I am." We are maybe more stepping backwards, more reserved maybe. Yeah. Show yourself. If you have the confidence and you know what you're capable of, like I said before, just show yourself. Write to a club and say, "I'm here. This is what I want."

Especially for youth – not only in the highest level, but also for youth. I think that would be really good. I have a lot of – not a lot of, but some – parents, and they not always understand the way man thinks, how they handle younger girls. I think we as a female could help our younger girls a lot to get more developed and get more challenge and more talent out of it, than we have now, in general.

I agree.

To finish up, I have two last questions. A reading list. You said you read a lot. Do you have any books that you would recommend people read?

I don't really have any recommendations. There are so many books. I mean it's just what you need. If you want to read something about the mental part, or the personal, or the management part, if you Google, then you will find a lot. I read a lot of articles.

Like scientific articles, you mean?

Yeah, I'm connected with social media, but I use it a lot to find articles. So on Twitter or Facebook, there are some postings and yeah, then I click on the article. Also, newspapers articles to read what's happening. They're changing a lot, every time. That's the way I'm keeping up and what I do. Like I said, of course sometimes I read a book, if I have the time. Most of the time, it's in the Summertime if I'm not working.

Okay. Last one. Do you have any advice for coaches who are just starting their career?

Yeah, go and watch the other coaches. Go and watch other practices. Maybe it's only for your colleague on the same level. And dare to ask questions. Go up to the head coach of the first team, or a different coach, and they will tell you if they can help you or not. You will learn a lot out of it, to watch different practices. Watch different kind of volleyball matches.

And watch people coaching, Maybe you're not hearing always how they coach, but you see their interaction and you can see the reaction of the players.

And try to read. Try to get some more information you can get, if you are interested. Yeah and you get, you take a little bit of something from everywhere.

Be yourself. Please, please don't copy someone. Don't copy. It's not possible. So get the best out of yourself.

Chapter Six

Denise Corlett

U.S. coach Denise Corlett is best know as an assistant and associate head coach for 31 years at Stanford University, though she was also involved in the USA national team program. During her tenure at Stanford they won nine NCAA championships and 18 PAC-10/PAC-12 titles. Denise was twice voted AVCA National Assistant Coach of the Year. She's known as one of the top recruiters in the game. If you talk to any player that has played for Denise, you hear about how she really values her relationship with them and how much care she has for them. Even after her Stanford career this really shines through. In this interview she talks about her recruiting process, her athlete-first philosophy, and the culture in place at Stanford. This interview was from a few months after she retired.

★★★

Could you start by telling us about your history and experience in volleyball?

I started volleyball when I was in grammar school. My mom was a P.E. teacher and grammar school coach, so I started playing the game probably when I was 10-11. I grew up in Manhattan Beach, California, a city very known for volleyball. So it was grammar school, high school, and then I played four years of volleyball at UCLA. I was on the U.S. National Team for about a year and a half until I got injured. And then from there I started working with junior teams. I was a software engineer for four and a half years, and then continued to stay involved with helping at UCLA. I eventually ended up north coaching at San Jose State for a year and a half, and Stanford for 31 years.

At least in Europe, I see that a lot of coaches get sucked into bigger and better, and struggle to settle down. You were there for 31 years at Stanford. What made you know it was the place for you, and that role that you wanted to be in?

Well, I'm from California. Never wanted to leave California was the first thing. Stanford is an amazing university. It's, I feel, one of the best, if not the best combination of athletics and academics, and I was very into the academic piece of things. I thought – for student-athletes – the main reason you're going to the university is to get an education. It just felt right. I just never had any... I never really looked for any jobs outside of California. I'm very close with my family. I had three nieces that all played collegiate volleyball, and I was able to be around when they grew up, watch them compete in high school and club. I got to see them a little bit during their college seasons. So that was part of it.

What was your role as Associate Head Coach?

I was mainly in charge of the recruiting. That was kind of my main job. But you did whatever you needed to do. Through the tenure I was there, sometimes I had setters. Sometimes I had defense. Sometimes I had blockers. So I probably did every role throughout the 31 years in terms of training of the teams.

Could you talk about you coaching influences? Whether it be initial or ongoing coaching influences that you had?

Obviously, my first coach was my mom. I learned a lot from her from the way she did things. And treated me like a player, not like her daughter, which was... There were times as a younger person that I didn't play, because she pretty much said I wasn't good enough. And I had to learn how to be a team player in that aspect. You know?

There's just so many people. I mean, Andy Banachowski is obviously one that I've played for and worked with after I was done. Another coach that wasn't volleyball that has been very influential in my life is Billie Moore. She was my basketball coach. I played basketball at UCLA, and she was the Olympic basketball coach in '76. I treasure her friendship still. We still keep in touch regarding stuff.

And just... I don't know. There are so many people that I was very fortunate to have played for, a lot of different coaches growing up. I had Gene Selznick as a coach. I had Harlan Cohen as a coach. Those are two names from the way past of people. I played for Arie Selinger. That was a tremendous coach. So those are people I got to play for.

And then getting to play with people like Flo Hyman, and Rita Crockett, and Debbie Green. That era. It was in that era with the National Team.

I can't pinpoint every coach, because there are just so many that have influenced me throughout the process. The three coaches I've worked for – Don Shaw and John Dunning and Kevin Hambly – they all had perspective with my growing different ways. So I always thank the three of them, also.

Coaching philosophy: How has that changed over time for you?

I think my main philosophy has always been, to me the kids are first. And that never changed. The things that changed through the years is the athleticism, the speed, the power that came into the game as you grew. And you tried to grow with that as a coach. But the main thing for me was caring about the kids, and making sure they were – as best you can – healthy in their mind and their body.

And again, at Stanford, making sure that they were able to move on with life. You know? They got their degrees, and they were able to... besides volleyball, I wanted to be there as a person. I was trying to – hopefully –

make sure that they were the best young women to go out of Stanford's door that they could be, and be successful in life on the court or off the court.

Are there a lot of differences between a training session from now and from when you started coaching?

Yeah. I mean, I think the tendency is geared more toward the men's style, a lot of it. You know? The blocking. You know? Everyone is training blocking now, which... I can date myself, but no one ran slides when I played. No one jump served. No one... I think we ran one-and-a-halves in the middle. And you just evolve as the game evolves, and put in your system.

And again, being an assistant coach, you kind of... The head coach made the decisions. You gave the input, but you kind of... All the three coaches I worked for all had different styles, and different strengths. What they thought was the priority differed. So you kind of go with, again, what I think my job as the assistant was – to develop your way to help each coach. But they had the way they wanted to do it, and you adapted to their style and gave input to any changes that you thought you could see.

On the two head coach changes you had while you were there, what was your role during that? And do you feel you had continuity in the role as the head coach changed?

Yeah. I mean, you changed. You know? Each head coach came in with different philosophies. I think they knew I was going to be loyal, and I was going to work hard, too. Because the priority wasn't me. The priority is the program, and the integrity of the program, and keeping that integrity of the program up and consistent. You know? You wanted to make sure that the transition was as seamless as you could make it for each coach and each team.

But the priority for the program was to compete for a national championship every year, and not see drops in that philosophy and in that way that the program was approached. I think for the transitions that was done. Stanford is a different place in that we were able to stay up in the top 10 for most of my tenure through the changes. Sometimes you don't see that when coaches change.

Do you have any idea what the keys were to staying in that top 10 for such a long time?

Well, the keys are the kids we got, obviously. They were all in it for the right reason. Like I said, to come to Stanford, you had to be a student first and an athlete near second. You wouldn't have been successful at Stanford if education was not as important or as equal to the volleyball.

And I think they all wanted to come in and continue the legacy that was built in the '80s and continue that. You know? You don't want to be that team that doesn't follow up with the legacy that Stanford had. It's one of the top legacies in the country in terms of the number of Final Fours, and the number of Championships. Every kid that came into the program wanted to be able to contribute to that legacy.

You've mentioned a couple of times the high value on academics at Stanford, as well as quite a good culture of success. So how did you, as a coach, help the athletes achieve and manage both areas?

One of the hard parts about Stanford is being admitted into the school. And a lot of my job in recruiting was talking through the admissions process. Because you have to get admitted into the university first. You have to fill out the application like everyone else does. Not every athlete that applies to Stanford gets admitted. You have to take the high-level classes, and you have to keep up the academic side. You know?

There was a number of student-athletes that we couldn't recruit to Stanford that would have helped us on the volleyball court. So you had to find that right person. And once they got there, they were going to be successful because they had those skills as high school kids. They had the skills of time management. They had the high priority. A lot of the students going to Stanford are taking APs and Honors classes, and are high achievers in the classroom before they got there.

So getting to Stanford was hard for them sometimes, because you're in a classroom with everyone else who's high achievers. And you don't have the time, sometimes, to do the same problem set. You might have three hours to do it, where other people in your class have six hours to do it. So you've got to find that balance and keep on top of things, versus just procrastinating, I guess, is the word. You know?

We probably averaged 3.5 a lot of times as a team [GPA]. In season, out of season. One of the things I've always prided myself on there was that we had 100% graduation rate. Every volleyball player that went to Stanford graduated. We had one player that didn't finish, that did not graduate from Stanford, so we never had a lot of transfers, either. They picked Stanford for the right reason. They all wanted to be successful, both on the volleyball court and off the volleyball court.

That leads me into a couple of other questions I was curious about. You were present for a couple of head coaches. What are your thoughts on culture development? And what was your role in it at Stanford? You have touched on it a little bit now, but let's get more specific.

Each team was different. You have different leaders. The main thing as coaches is the culture we wanted to try to create was that the team was first. And you're here for not just yourself. You're here representing your university. You're here representing your teammates. So everything you do is aligned with what you do off the court outside the gym. You know?

The thing with Stanford Athletics is that it's very successful in a lot of sports. So you're looked up to on campus as an athlete. But there's a lot of good athletes there. The class that just finished their senior year last year, in their freshman class they had five people that had already been in the Olympics coming in as freshmen. So there's a lot of expectations, not just on the volleyball court, but for a lot of Stanford athletes.

And it's a very funny, supportive place, because one out of seven, maybe one out of eight, students at Stanford is a student-athlete of some kind. It's a really small school in terms of population. But you're surrounded by so many people that are doing the same thing you are. You know? Katie Ledecky [swimmer] is in your class. You got Andrew Luck, who was a number one draft choice of the NFL a few years ago. His sister was on our team.

And you have relationships with those people as a coach. It was such a great environment, because you had Olympic coaches on your staff. You know? So you're surrounded by a lot of people doing everything that you want to do.

The whole culture of the school is just one of excellence.

Yeah. Like I said, it was an amazing place. That's why I stayed there. It was pretty fun.

How do you go about finding players that just fit that culture?

Well, I've probably talked to more or as many high school counselors than I did coaches. Because you can see what you can see on the court. And you can figure out who you want to recruit in terms of athletic ability. You know?

So the other thing I would watch a lot is how they reacted, how they treated their teammates, how they treated their coaches. You observe a lot of that while you're watching them play. And how do they celebrate when they do something well? How do they celebrate when they don't do something well? And the same thing with their teammates.

So that was a big thing for me – how they were as people. And then the academic piece, you just had to find out information, because they had to be taking the right classes. If they weren't taking Honors and APs, even as a top-level athlete, you might not get admitted to Stanford. You want to get to Stanford and be able to be successful in the classroom, and not be at risk as a student. You don't want to bring anyone at risk that would struggle. And so you just have to continue to get as much academic information as you can.

And then when you're talking to the student-athletes and their families in the recruiting process. After you've been there a while, you can tell the ones that really had the drive. And you can tell the ones that... maybe you weren't sure. You know?

There were some kids if you asked them to change their classes, tweak their classes a little bit, and they were like, "Okay. What else?" Or you have a, "I'm not really sure I want to do that." And then you would kind of know sometimes that maybe this is too hard. You have kids that have dreams to go to Stanford that maybe academically couldn't. And you don't want to bring them into a place where they're not going to be successful once they get there. That's important.

Those initial things that you said you were looking at as well – how they act with their teammates, and coaches, and things like that – do you talk to them about that when they arrive? That there were things that you liked, and reasons they were recruited?

Yeah. I mean, you talk to them about it in the recruiting process as you get to know them. I was fortunate to be able to recruit really good players. And so you want to make sure you get the good piece that goes with the good player. You go to college and are surround by stars. You're a star on your club team, but you might not play at some of the colleges. So you talk to them about that.

I remember sitting down way back when we had four freshmen starting as freshmen. And the next year's class, we pointed it out and said, "Are you okay with all this? You have four kids starting as a freshman that won the National Championship. You have to come in and compete. Can you come in and compete for the job?"

Because we never a promised a kid that, "You're going to start." They had to earn it. And it's something that you earn in practice. You earn with the respect of your teammates, and you have to find the balance where you have the players that don't get the limelight, that don't play all the time, that are working as hard as the other kids on the court every day and don't get the accolades that some players get. Are they the right people that aren't going to bring the team down? Because that's the thing that can hurt a team. Any dissension or any player that's unhappy can bring your team down with them.

How did you manage that with the players that aren't getting as much court time? Was it just a front loading, and, "This is not going to happen this year?"

I think it's just talk – communicating, making sure they understood their roles, and doing the best you can to help them in their pursuit to continue to greatness. You're just there to help and do the best you can. Again, the team was first. And understanding that, and just managing personalities. But communication is the key.

That sort of philosophy of recruitment, did that change with different head coaches? Or did that stay the whole way through?

No, because for me, you're recruiting to the school. The coaches are there to coach the team. But you had to get the right people into the school. You know? So maybe a kid changed here or there what that coach liked differently in an athlete, versus another coach. But you still had to make sure they fit the academics.

I haven't had the pleasure yet to coach any Stanford athletes, but I played with a couple and against a couple. Their feedback to me was about you would always be your ability to maintain relationships through the recruiting phase to the athlete phase, and then to the alumni phase. How do you manage that differently? And how do you keep connection?

I just like them. I call them, "My kids." They're all my kids. I have a lot of kids. And I just care about all of them for who they are. And I hope I'll always be able to stay in touch. That's probably the thing I'll miss, is the relationships I had or were able to get as you go through the process. You know?

My goal was always just to be able to be a positive part of their life, and someone that they could trust, and someone that they can contact if they need anything. You try to stay out of their life. It's their life. I wanted to be someone that they can fall back on if they needed any advice.

I can imagine that in such a high sort of performing environment, for the player to have someone who genuinely cares about them as a person, too, is pretty important.

Yeah.

So if you were to give advice to upcoming coaches on how to be a great recruiter, what's the most important thing?

Probably be patient in the process. Be honest in the process. And communicate as well as you can with them. I would say don't tell them what they need to hear, but tell them what they should hear. Because I did Juniors for a number of years, and there's a lot of kids that went through the process that I coached that… You're listening to them talk about these schools, and you're kind of going, "I'm not sure that's the way it is." You know?

I'd say trust your process. Trust where you coach. Trust what you're talking about. And like I said, communicate as best as you can. It's all about communication.

So it's less about selling…

I always said I didn't want to be a salesman. I wanted to be an information getter. So if you needed some information about something at Stanford, let me know what it is. But I wasn't going to sell you on Stanford. I was fortunate: Stanford sold itself in a lot of ways. And people will say that.

A lot of people said I had the easy job, because I was recruiting for Stanford. The hard part was finding the right pieces that could fit all the academic puzzle there.

I mean, I had a coach one time say, "You never talk about volleyball," when I was recruiting. And I said, "Well, volleyball is such an added bonus." There are so many things at Stanford that made it why you come to Stanford. You talk about that. You talk about the opportunities they get as student athletes: The careers they could get, the alumni connections that they could make. You know?

I mean, Franci [Girard] was one who benefited from being in the right spot at the right time for a job. And in terms of her first job, in Goldman Sachs, I think it was. I don't know if she told you this story [Lauren and Franci were teammates], but she was talking to a donor. We had gone to their house and she knew, I think, the President or the CEO. And Franci met them right there. The way Franci was as a person, she clicked with these people. And all of a sudden, she was offered a job.

So I mean, there's just so many things that can happen that I talked about that more than even the volleyball part. Because volleyball was a given. They were going to be good players, and we were going to have good teams, and we were going to be successful.

Moving around forward a little, did you guys do any specific team-building activities? Do you believe in it?

We did different ones. We did a couple ropes courses. We did a couple scavenger hunts. Like I said, every team was different. Every group was different. You try to tailor it to each group. You know?

I think a lot of the team-building for me was their own personal team-building where they had to figure out how to build within their own peers, and not, sometimes, be driven by the coaches. The coaches, for the most part, are involved. But I think the team, they're the ones that have to bond. They're the ones that live the dream. They're the ones in that locker room. They're the ones controlling the speak.

So I always felt that the team-building part for me was team-driven, player-driven. Each year, like I said, was a different thing that you tried to do. You try to vary it. The ropes courses were fun. They liked doing that stuff. And like I said, the scavenger hunts were... We did one where you rode in a kayak, and then you tried to figure out this puzzle. And there were some that were emotional, and some that weren't emotional. And so there's just all different ways to do it, and each team was different.

Did you encourage or facilitate that personal team-building at all?

I was there if I needed to. I usually wasn't the one that was in charge of all that, because that's your head coaches. You know what I'm saying? And like I said, I think for me, the one I encouraged was the personal relationships between each other.

I encouraged that a lot.

Little things like how to talk to each other on the court, how to play with each other. Does everyone know something about everybody? You know? And you can't lead by... You have to learn to lead by it, because it's all taken by how it's interpreted, or how it's said. You have to make sure, if you're a leader, you say it in the right way. That's not necessarily your way, but the way the team will accept it.

And sometimes, being harsh. Sometimes, being honest. Sometimes, being... You know? I encouraged the main leaders of the team to make sure they got to know every person on the team individually as a person, not just as a volleyball player.

And you'd help them through that process a little bit as well, yeah?

Yeah.

So then the leadership and captain selection: What are your thoughts on selecting captains, and what their roles are?

Again, I'd say each group is different. And each coach has been different. Some coaches I've dealt with, sometimes we voted, sometimes we didn't. Sometimes the coach assigned. One of the coaches I worked with did it four different ways, Just because it was the way the team did it.

And some teams didn't have any captains. The leadership comes out as you go, and without assigning a title. We had a captain one year of a... One of our best leaders was a girl that never played. And she was one of the best captains, because she controlled the emotions of the players and was that person.

So yeah, I don't think you can have a certain way to do it. I think you have to take each season and each year. One of our best leaders became a captain as a sophomore because she evolved as a team leader. But she was probably more the leader on the court versus the leader in the locker room. And like I said, there's different leaders in that aspect.

So most of it, for me, is you kind of let it evolve. And even the junior teams that I've coached over the years where I was the head coach have done it different ways in terms of divvying up duties.I mean, different people going and taking leadership roles so they learn that role, giving them responsibility so they learn that role also.

Could you give us a bit deeper examples of a couple of those?

Of different roles?

Yeah.

Like I said, you have the leader on the court. So you have the captain on a court, which – depending on who that could be – who has got to have the volleyball savvy to know when to approach the refs and when not to approach the refs. You have to have the team mom. That's probably a leadership role within the team. You have to have someone that gets on them to put their stuff away in the locker room.

You have to have the team listener, someone that's there to be that listens. Sometimes you have to have someone that gets on them for not doing their jobs as a team player. You know?

I think those are probably the main ones. Again, each person is different in how they lead. And I think the thing that's most important is the way you lead has got to be you, but the way you lead has got to be interpreted and accepted by your teammates. So if you lead by example, you've got to do it every day. There's a lot of people that do that – lead by example. Some people are silent leaders that don't say a word.

I know of someone – I didn't play with her or coach her – that was probably one of the best leaders in the country and in the National Team level, and I don't think she ever said a word on the court. But the team knew what she was doing. All she had to do was look at them in the eye, and they respected that.

So again, you have to find your way to be that leader. My leadership, the way I would do it is different than I would ask anyone else to do it, because they're all different. You'd give them your perspective after observing them and talking to them about it, but everyone has got to find their own way to be a leader.

I am jumping around a lot on topics here, but could you talk about how you guys manage different phases of the season, whether it be pre-season or heading into the tournament, for example? Whether it be training, match preparation, and that kind of stuff?

We would come in, kind of start in August, and everyone has about the four to five weeks of training. The positive for us, in different ways, is we weren't in school. So we were able to take trips when our pre-season hit.

So you kind of have different seasons. You have the double days, and fall camp, and whatever way you want to call that version where you've got four to five weeks of practicing. And then you have your pre-season [pre-conference] tournaments, which is usually four weeks. And you schedule that where you schedule that.

And because of our schooling situation, we were allowed to travel. So we did some 10-day road trips. Sometimes we did local. Sometimes we did far away. Sometimes we just picked places. One year, we picked Boston because we'd never been to Boston. So we called the Boston coaches and set up a tournament in Boston. And the girls got to go sightseeing, and got to go to a Red Sox game. And a couple of times, we've been to Washington D.C. And you take a couple days where you can explore, because obviously, they were very into the exploring part and the educational pieces of that.

And then you have your conference, which, for PAC-12, is very demanding. And by that time, we're in school. So now you're balancing the school aspect with the volleyball aspect.

Then your next season is your post-season. And planning for that ahead, because most likely, we're in finals during some part of the post-season. So you're planning that part of the piece of possibly being gone during finals week, and managing your academics during that time. So that's August through December.

We're a quarter system school. That means we have four quarters in Fall, Winter, Spring, and then the Summer. Our quarters are 10 weeks long, and then a final week. So about 11 weeks, plus Spring Break. During the Winter quarter a lot of times – and sometimes it's changed – we would have that as kind of our down quarter where we would use our eight hours a week most of the time. You're about 20 hours in your season, and eight hours of non-traditional [When Denise says non-traditional here she's referring to the time outside the regular and Spring seasons].

We would use that time in the Winter quarter where the student athletes could take whatever classes they would like, and we would work around their academic schedule so they could take some things they might not be able to take during the season because we have practice during that time. And then our Spring quarter we'd usually go back to six or seven weeks of our 20-hour a week training in that time. So that's how we broke it up.

And we didn't require summer school. So we never have a lot of kids around during the summer. A lot of them would come back and work camp, but most of them would either get an internship, or go home, or do something in terms of a job-related activity.

How did the training week change?

It all changed depending on the schedule. We had years where, before TV got involved, you had Friday-Saturday games. Then, as things got bigger, you went to Friday-Sunday games so you didn't conflict with football. Things like that. Because it's hard to have a volleyball game when you're trying to get people in the seats – and now you have season tickets – when you have football, because you're talking staff.

And then TV came in, and we started having Wednesday night games if you were picked for it. So then the schedule got kind of wacky when you played Wednesday-Fridays, or Thursday-Saturdays, or a couple times we did a Wednesday-Sunday. You know? Just, again, TV kind of dictated that.

So over the last couple of years, I think most of the games were Friday-Sundays. Because the new rules that came in a couple years ago that travel days were not allowed to be off-days, if you played Sunday afternoon and got home, you had to take Monday off from volleyball. So a lot of times, Mondays were off. And then you trained Tuesday, Wednesday, Thursday. But then, sometimes you traveled on Thursday to leave for the next place on Friday, and then practiced on Saturday, and played on Sunday.

So every week was different. You tried to get at least three good days of practice in a week preparing for the two matches you had on the weekend. And then the first time through the PAC-12 it's learning. The second time through, it's a little easier, because obviously, you've played everybody once. A lot of people know each other because they've been in the league. The seniors probably know everybody in the conference, because they've been playing for three years. Kind of like the pros, where you get to know your league there.

Each coach has a different philosophy. Sometimes lift three times a week. For sure, two times a week in the season. Sometimes one coach had a philosophy of lifting a little bit every day. Game day, also. So there's different ways that that training is done, but you want to make sure you get your strength & conditioning going. And then our Winter quarter was where you build it back up in strength conditioning.

Because Summer... Like I said, we don't require summer school. So a lot of kids are on their own for their training purposes.

What about game preparation with the team with the scouting, and video, and things like that? How would you guys prepare with the team?

Kids can watch a lot on their own. We didn't mandate how much you had to watch. We just expected that they wanted to be prepared. Probably the last 15 years, I'd say, as a team, we would spend no more than between half hour to an hour as a team watching film. And everything else was pretty much on your own. Kids can watch it on their phones. There's just so much more accessibility that you can watch matches. You can pull up by a hitter and watch tendencies. So I know Morgan, our libero, would pull up hitters and watch where she thought the ball was going to be, and where the block was. And so I think that's something that is... as part of the learning process, and learning to be a student of the game... we just encouraged them to watch as much video as they could fit in their schedule.

I know some coaches would track what kids were watching. And you always knew when it was midterm time when they came into the scouting meetings and they weren't as prepared because they were probably coming in from a midterm. So those are different things, too. You got to think about all that, because there's different things going on in their lives besides just volleyball.

So if you're heading into the Final Four tournament, then the girls are getting a scouting sheet and having to prepare for a meeting beforehand? Is that sort of how you do that? And then jumped into it in training, and ran through some things?

Yeah. We would try to probably scout the day before we played.

As coaches, you knew on Monday kind of what you were going to prepare for, so you try to put those things into the mix. You know?

If you played... I mean, there was years where USC ran this really high ball, and UCLA ran a really fast ball. And we're preparing for both of those in the same week. So you picked your battles on what you wanted to work on.

You kind of started... not really giving them a scouting report, but they knew what was happening at practice. How you did things at practice was kind of starting to prepare them for the week, and different ways of what that [opposing] team was like. And like I said, most of them already knew, because they had already looked at them themselves.

Is there other ways that you're integrating stats or technology into the program?

Kevin, the most recent coach, was very into the stats. He looked at stats during the game. John wasn't so much a stat guy. He was a pencil and paper type-guy. He was a math major, so he was into numbers.

Don, back in the day, I don't think we had stats. I mean, I think you had some, but it wasn't computer-generated. He spent most of his time making tapes, because that's how you had to do it back in the day. It was do-it-yourself.

And so again, you've seen the different things. But everyone uses stats in different ways. Some people are very dependent on them in matches, and some people are not. I was probably in between. You know? I wasn't a true stat person on the bench, but I looked at the numbers.

I heard... I don't even know where I read it. I guess there was a wellness survey that the girls were completing the last couple years?

Yeah. Kevin brought that in. It was just more to see how they were doing on each day as best as you can. You know? Are they getting enough sleep?

It wasn't to check up on them. It was just to give more of a resource for them to kind of fall back on, also. And just wanted to make sure if you didn't get enough sleep that you talked to him about what's going on, or if you saw red flags. And so you had some things to help them with if they were struggling with the other things besides volleyball.

Was that mandatory for them to fill in, or optional?

It was recommended. That was it.

Okay. So as coaches, we need to be pretty knowledgeable in a lot of areas, whether it be technical, tactical, or even personal. What do you think are the most important qualities for coaching?

Well, for me, I would say personal. That's my priority, was the personal part.

I think tactical was my next strength, probably. I loved the tactical part. As a setter, pulling those middles. And as a hitter, showing this and doing that, things like that.

And then technical is there, but by the time we get them in college, I think you're... I call it "tweaking." You're not really changing. You might be changing some... a lot... but you're not really changing, especially when they come in as freshmen. You're just kind of adding to their game versus changing their game. And I think that's the difference. But I think the first two are the priorities, or my priorities were personal, then tactical, then technical.

What was your tactical role during the game? Did that change depending on the head coach?

No. The one that kind of stayed consistent was I always took the other team's serve receive and tendencies. Probably because I had done that. I started charting... probably for Andy back in 1980 [at UCLA]. So I just always kind of did that. I'm not sure why.

But like I said, sometimes I called serves. Sometimes I called blocks. Sometimes I'd change the defense. Sometimes I called offense. I've had different roles with different coaches and different teams.

Favorite parts of coaching?

Relationships.

Simple.

Yep. Simple answer.

Looking back, what are some mistakes you've made and things you've learned, or changes you've made from the mistakes that you've made?

I don't know. That's a tough one. I don't know what to say on that one. Not that I haven't made mistakes, but there's not much I would change, because I thought I did pretty well in keeping my job through three coaches, and the trust they had in me, and the loyalty that I showed to Stanford and the program.

I guess that would follow into our next question. It's a pretty simple one: What makes a good assistant coach?

Knowing your role. I think knowing your role, and making sure your voice is heard at the right times, and in the right places, and the right place. Always understanding the head coach is in charge. And giving feedback to what you want to do, but do it the right way, and do it at the right time.

Know you have a say, but it's how and when you make the say. You know? You have to understand that they're in charge, and everything you want to say might not get heard. It might get heard, but it might not get implemented. And you have to be okay with that.

I'd actually like to talk a little bit about your work with the Team USA teams: Some experiences you've had, and dive a little bit deeper into that. Could you talk us through some experiences you had with Team USA?

Yeah. I haven't been involved in a number of years. I probably started when I played. Even when I was on the team, I was probably the 13th, 14th player. And we had a team manager that had left, so I kind of helped take over those roles when I was a player back in the '80s.

Then most of the roles I've had were kind of the team leaders, which is more of the team manager. So I think having the trust of the head coaches, going in and helping at tournaments. I went to four World Championships for Juniors with different coaches.

And I think the USA program trusted me in helping the coaches do their roles. You know? You could go in that role and not be a coach, but you'd be there to facilitate the laundry, and make sure they had their water, and kind of be the one behind the scenes. I never liked to be in front, in the forefront. I've always liked to be behind. So it was a perfect role for me in that aspect.

But having USA on your back is just a feeling that you don't get very often unless you're sitting there watching your team compete. And being part of that all of a sudden when they play your anthem and representing your country is one of the best things you can ever do, playing or coaching.

Yep. I agree with that.

What do you think the barriers are to getting more female coaches in the spotlight and better represented?

Some of them are family oriented, I would say. I'm not... I don't have kids. College coaching, it takes you away a lot to recruit in timing during the season. So I think that could be part of it. You know?

I'm not sure what the other answers are. A lot of our kids don't go on to coach because they go on to other things in their lives. It could be a financial situation. You know? I mean, I look back when I was a software engineer, and the money I made then. If I was in coaching at that time... that was night and day.

Then you're talking... On a weekend for recruiting, you're in a gym from 8:00 AM to maybe 8:00 PM for two and a half days. And you're not home. I'm hoping some of this COVID stuff that came out, the positives of it that... I mean, I heard coaches that haven't been home for Easter or someone's birthday for 10 years, and all of a sudden they were home. So I hope that the coaches can sit back and realize you can get the job done and not be on the go so much.

And I think some of the positives, also, with the COVID is the Zoom calls that now. I think you can generate more things that'll happen in terms of connecting with recruits and the other people on your staff without having to be physically in the office every single day. One of our players who works at Google, she doesn't know when she'll go back, because Google has got to change all their operations because they all were in one room. And now they've got to have the social distancing.

So I think it doesn't really answer your question on why there are not enough females. But I think those are two of them. It's a big time commitment. And you have to do it for the love of the game, because it's not always the highest paid job if you're looking at making money. But you can help a lot of kids. You can be part of people's lives, and generate a lot of support for these people as they're growing up. And that's the part that I thrive. You see a lot of people that do it for the good of the kids, the good of the sport.

There's just a lot of time in anything you do. But coaching takes a lot of time away from your family life. I've known people who never got to see their kids play in college because they couldn't go.

I know when I worked with John Dunning I was like, "You have to go once to watch." His daughter played for four years on the opposite coast, and I think he saw her once a year to play in-person. So that's hard. You know? That's a tough thing sometimes.

That's quite a common answer. I'm just curious if that coaching paradigm can change a little bit, because eventually there's a better way.

Well, I think we're slowing the recruiting process down, hopefully... which they did last year, where you don't have to spend... I mean, you hopefully don't have to spend as many hours in the gym watching 14s and 15s, because the kids that you were worried about that were going to commit as eighth graders and ninth graders, now you have time where you have to watch them evolve as people.

I was never for the early commitments, because the way you are at 14... You're going to be different at 17 as a person. And what you think is fun there... I mean, I remember taking a kid. We had a kid come in for camp one year, and it was an eighth grader. It was one of the top eighth graders. And she was more worried about what hair clip she had in her hair than wanting to hear about Stanford. You know? The parents wanted to hear about Stanford.

So I hope that in this process of slowing that down, it can slow down the coaches. And part of the rules that they've put into the college... especially volleyball over the last few years... it's supposed to be for quality of life in terms of doing that. I mean, I was one of the persons that put in the first recruiting calendar. I don't even know when that was. But it took five years because of all the different ideas.

I had one coach come up and say, "I don't like this. I want to be the last person in the gym. I want to be able to go when I want. I want that kid to know that I'm there every single time, that I really want them." And I said to her, "You know, that's great." She was just probably her first or second year into coaching. I said, "Talk to me in 10 years from now when you're married with kids and tell me what you think of these rules."

And the rules finally went in. And after six months, she called me and said, "I get it now. I'm starting to get it now. I have a weekend home." And I had coaches that, at the beginning, thanked people. Because they said, "I can actually be home on a weekend and not think about, 'I should be out on the road,' because everyone else is out on the road. And I could actually relax with my family and enjoy some family time."

I think that that's part of the things that has to come into play, is that these coaches have to understand that it is a quality of life. And don't burn yourself out! I'm at the end of my career, so I can say that now. But it takes a lot of toll. You know? Like I said, most of the reason I decided to get out was so I could have more family time.

I missed work days. My mom had some health issues, had a scare in December during the playoffs. And not being able to see her for a week and a half because I was busy with my schedule... because I was in the playoffs... that was hard. I was very close to my nieces, and my youngest one has just had her second little boy. And I want to be able to be at birthdays, and go down, and not just see them twice a year. When we would go to LA, I'd maybe see them for five minutes.

Again, it probably took me 20 years to figure that part out. Because I was the one that went to the gym all day, and worked hard, and did everything I could to get the kids there, and to make sure they knew what my job was about.

I just... The thing I can say is just slow down a little bit. With the kids slowing down, I hope the world can slow down. And volleyball can slow down a little bit, too.

That's so interesting. I've been doing a lot of thinking about men versus women. I coached men's volleyball as well before I moved into women's coaching. And just in general, something I've seen is that... I don't like to generalize, but as women, we tend to think a little bit more about the quality of life side of the factor as well, which immediately pushes you away from coaching. So that's why I wonder if that paradigm of coaching has changed a little bit and encouraged more women to get involved.

I don't know how I would be if I was married and had kids. I don't know. I don't know what I would have done different. I probably wouldn't have done it different, because I would go, and I wouldn't want to be at things. You know?

I was fortunate. When my nieces played club, I found out their schedules and I tried to make sure my recruiting schedule revolved around their tournaments as best as I could so I could be there. I was able to watch them. I was close enough to where I lived that I could go watch them play in high school. But there were different parameters there. Technically, I wasn't allowed to go to things because I wasn't their parent. I was just their aunt. You know? So I didn't jeopardize anything that would hurt my recruiting. To jeopardize my job. You know?

But I remember going to... There was one event on one of my niece's... They had won their sectional tournament. And my sister was like, "Come to the after party!" And I said, "I can't. I'm not allowed to go to those things."

So I ended up going. And for the first half hour, I sat outside by myself. And then I finally went in, and it ended up being four people on my niece's team whose parents I had gone to grammar school with. So I said, "Okay. I'm comfortable with these people." There was a pre-existing relationship because I had gone to grammar school with them. My mom was their PE teacher. So I went in and actually was a normal person.

But you know? You're kind of like, "Can I be a normal person and be an aunt supporting your niece playing her biggest matches?" Because you were a coach at a college that wasn't allowed to go in the gym. I missed some things that I wish that I didn't miss. So if I had my own kids, I don't know what I'd be doing right now. If it was... It would be different.

Have there been any challenges that you've faced that you would say are unique to female coaches?

No. I mean, I... No, not really. I think you work hard. You earn your pay. You earn what you're doing. You try to get respect, I think, female or male. I mean, I think I tried to get the respect of people because I was a hard worker. And I was very trusting, and very loyal, and very honest. And so I don't think I... I didn't make challenges for myself.

Are there any stereotypes or misunderstandings about female coaches that you would like to clear up or argue against?

No. I just think we're as capable as everyone else. I mean, you have to earn it. You can't get a job because you're a female. You have to earn the job because you're a good coach, and you're a good person.

I think that's the hard part. We do need more female coaches. I don't think there's enough. The pool is not big enough, I don't think, in a lot of ways. It's getting bigger. There's more coaches, I think, in the last number of years that are going into coaching. So there's a lot. The pool is bigger. But the pool when I came into coaching... there weren't a lot of females doing it.

And I don't know why. You know? If you look at the numbers, there's more women's basketball coaches in the world, I think. You know? Why is that? I don't know. It could be a financial thing. They make more money. That's for sure! The high-powered female women's coaches, they're making... I don't know. Half a million dollars they could be making, some of them [In college basketball the top earners are getting multi-millions].

But that's just the world. Football coaches are going to make a lot of money. Men's basketball coaches are going to make a lot of money. But they also... They're the ones that generate the funds at colleges. And you have to support them, because unfortunately, that's the way the world is. You know? There's 50,000 people at football games, and there's 2,000 at volleyball games.

Let's get more in the seats. But you've got to have the money for marketing. There's just more people. There's more involved now in college. You've got marketing, and you have promotions, and you have season tickets. And it's probably been in the last 10, 15 years that that's all of a sudden been evolving for the women's side... women's volleyball... whereas, obviously, men's basketball and football has been for years.

Okay. I've got two more questions for you. First, do you have any books that you'd recommend?

You know, I'm not a big reader. I'll just say that. I mean, I love to read. But I don't have a list. So sorry about that.

No problem at all. And to finish off... Do you have any advice for coaches that are starting their career?

Work hard. Put in the time. You can't snap your fingers and make it go. You've got to work hard.

Learn everything about the aspect of your program. So just don't want to be in the gym. There is so much more to college coaching, at least, that is outside the gym. I think a lot of coaches going in just want to be in the practice gym, and train, and do that. But if you want to be a coach in the future, you got to learn everything. You got to learn the academic side. You got to learn the marketing side. You've got to do as best as you can on the budget side.

Over the years, when we've had brand new coaches coming out of college, they're like, "Oh, my God! I have to be in the office this much? I didn't know this was what it was about." It was mostly, "I just want to... Can I just go to gym? And can I just bang the balls?" And so that's probably it.

Chapter Seven

Bonus: Jenny McDowell

Jenny McDowell took over the program at Division III Emory University in 1996 and coached there through the 2022 season, after which she stepped down. In those 27 seasons she won 2 NCAA championships, 10 conference titles, and over 800 matches. Her players earned 52 All-American and 85 All-Region selections. John interviewed Jenny during the first round of Wizards interviews. When thinking about who she should put on her to-interview list, Lauren reviewed Jenny's interview and decided there probably wasn't a need to redo it. To celebrate Jenny's outstanding career, we're including that conversation as a bonus, even though it doesn't follow the by women, for women model of the rest of the interviews here. Note that we did exclude a section that got into some nitty gritty details around recruiting along with some other extraneous conversation that, while relevant at the time, is dated now.

***

First thing I usually ask is just for you to talk through your coaching biography.

Sure. Just real quick, I grew up in Pennsylvania and then I was recruited to the University of Georgia, so I ended up going to play there. Then I became a GA there. I'm not sure if you know the name Jim Iams, but he was the national team assistant under Terry Liskevych. He came in right when I was about to start grad school, so he asked me to join his staff. I coached with him for, I think it was seven years at the University of Georgia, and Jim and I coached together the entire time. Thankfully he connected me and I did a few things with he and the USA team. Then in '96, this job at Emory opened up and everybody thought I was absolutely crazy to leave Georgia and not go the Division I route. In '96, I decided to come to Emory and I've been here ever since. I've been to two places and loved both of them and I'm starting my 20th season this year.

Okay, that's interesting. A northern girl finds her home in the south.

Yeah, I know it's crazy. I thought about staying up there at Pitt or Penn State, or one of those areas. Then I came and visited the South and loved it, and haven't left.

You can kind of hear a little bit of it in your voice now. You've definitely picked up a little. Not full on southern but there's a little bit there.

A little bit. I'm not sure if that's a good thing or a bad thing.

Me neither. All right, you talked a little bit about your coaching influence, or one of your coaching influences. Who's helped you out along the way in terms of your development?

I put Kathy DeBoer up there pretty high. Kathy, as you know, is the Executive Director of the AVCA. She was at Kentucky when I was at Georgia and I did a lot of different things with her - camps and clinics. We've stayed really, really good friends, so she's been a great mentor for me. Teri Clemens, one of the great mentors in my life. She coached at Washington University in St. Louis, won seven straight national champions. She's been huge in my development as well. Then again, I spoke to Jim Iams - got to train with him for quite a long time. I think in a roundabout way Russ Rose has been a mentor for me. Growing up in Pennsylvania, he's helped me a lot through my career at Georgia and at Emory. He's come down here, done the Art of Coaching clinic here, and he's always been a major supporter of me and going the Division III route. I would say those four have had a huge influence.

It's interesting to hear you talk about people that - except in one case - you didn't actually work with directly. How did it come to pass that you became connected with the likes of Kathy and Teri and developed that mentor mentee type of relationship?

With Kathy, I worked in a lot of her camps during the Summer. I knew that I wanted to be around Kathy as much as I could, and she was the head coach at that point. I really consider myself a sponge in a lot of ways. I thought she was one of the great coaches in the country at the time. I did all that I could to spend time with her and do her camps and do her clinics. We stayed very connected since she's been with the AVCA. I even wrote a book with Teri Clemens because Kathy asked us to do that. We spent a couple years coming up with the drill book that the AVCA promoted. Throughout my coaching career, I just stayed really connected with her.

With Russ, when I was growing up in Pennsylvania I also attended a lot of his camps. He knew of me. We laugh because I think I was considering Penn State but I don't think Penn State was considering me. He's been great. A home town kid, he's continued to watch my career. I see him on the road recruiting a lot and we'll talk a lot. Again, through the coaching clinic when he spent time here we just stayed connected that way and he always says, "Whatever you need." He's been a great mentor for me.

Then Teri Clemens was in my conference. When I came to Emory she was still coaching at Washington University in St. Louis and took me under her wing. She's become one of my best friends.

Probably lastly, Sharon Dingman, who was the coach at Iowa and now is the coach at University of Chicago. Again just a great colleague, great friend who we bounced a lot of ideas off of.

I think that's part of the coaching world in volleyball, in that you need to find those colleagues that also become mentors - even through you're not working side by side with them.

You said you started off as a GA. What was that experience like?

Yeah, I was getting my Masters at the time. I knew it was really important for me to get my Masters and Jim Iams was amazing and supported that - trying to juggle a bunch of different things. I didn't know if I wanted to go into the business world or if I wanted to go into coaching. That allowed me to do both things at the time. I was juggling a lot of things but I also knew Jim was supporting that. Jim had played at Stanford, so he understood how important education was and was just a great influence for me from the educational standpoint. Once I was done with that, he just said, "Hey, the first assistant position is open." He offered that to me and we became partners for six years and had some great years when I was in the full-time position.

Presumably, some of the players on the team when you GA were your former teammates, correct?

That is correct.

What was it like coaching your old teammates?

It was fine. It was actually really positive because when I was a player, I was definitely a leader type personality. I was the setter and I was captain. I was a leader to begin with. That's just my personality. I knew that Jim was the ultimate decision- maker. We had another assistant, Julie Herman, who's actually the Director of Athletics at Rutgers now. We had two great and powerful people, so I was able to be that liaison between the two, and it was actually a really positive experience.

You didn't run into any issues where your prior relationships caused any sort of conflict or potential challenges?

No, I didn't. Or at least I don't remember.

Emory is one of the more academic schools, for those who don't really know the structure. It must have it's own set of challenges in terms of recruiting and athlete retention and all those things. What framework from that perspective do you have to work in?

Great question. It's one of the top 20 academic universities in the country. I'm just super thankful there's a lot of very intelligent volleyball players out there that I'm able to recruit. When we start the recruiting process, obviously the priority is will they fit the academic profile of Emory? Our average ACT is 31 to 33, our GPA is 3.7 to 3.9, and then our SAT is similar, obviously, to the ACT correspondingly. I have to look at that first. We have to look at that before we can even begin the recruiting process with them. Once we do that, then the next step is can they play at the level that we play.

People have a misconception about Division III, in that the volleyball - because it has that Division III stigma on it - that the volleyball is not very good. Every single player on our team had multiple Division I offers. They were just looking for a university that was a top 20 academic school.

When you combine those two, yes it filters out a lot of players that are playing out there. But on the other hand, we're fortunate that volleyball does attract some very smart kids. Once we go through it and look at their academic profile, we're able to narrow it down to people that fit.

The other thing is they have to be passionate about the academics. Even if they have outstanding grades, they still have to be passionate about it. Because once you get to Emory - or a school like Brown, like you worked at - they're going to have to work really hard and to be successful. They're going to have to be passionate about their academics. We have to find that out about the student athlete as well.

I can tell you, I absolutely love this environment. I love working with really smart kids that have dreams to become doctors and lawyers, and getting their MBAs and running companies, and things like that. I love to be around this type of student athletes.

I can appreciate that. For those who don't know, can you describe the calendar for you in terms of when you have the kids. When you're allowed to work with them and when you're not allowed to work with them?

Sure, great question. Our pre-season, you can have 16 practice opportunities before the first date of competition. You have to count back in the calendar. This coming year, we're able to start practicing August 19th. Our players will come in August 18th and then we'll start practicing August 19th. You'll have the pre-season based on when your first day of class is. Usually you only get approximately a week of 2-a-days because of the first day of class. Once classes start, we practice 3:00 to 6:30, we don't go any longer than that, because obviously they have pressure of the academics here. We thankfully finish up the weekend before Thanksgiving, if we make it to the finals. The Division III National Finals are the weekend before Thanksgiving. Once that is over, I do not see the player or can practice with them other than five weeks during the spring.

You can have 16 practice/play opportunities [in the Spring] - meaning you can practice 15 times, you can play one time. You can choose when that's going to be throughout your second semester. We like to go three times a week for five weeks and then we usually host one tournament. Then after that, we won't see them again until the pre-season begins. Any of the strength and conditioning and weight training has to be on a volunteer basis and on their own. That's another reason why I have to recruit passionate kids that want to stay fit and want to stay in shape and are motivated to play on their own. Because if I don't, those kids obviously won't continue to play at the high level that our team plays at.

How big a roster do you tend to carry?

We carry anywhere from 16 to 22. That may seem big, but as you know, you've been in a similar situation, a lot of our kids are pre-med or doing different things. I like to train quite a bit 6-on-6. We have quite a few players that come late to practice or have to leave early based on labs, based on internships.

So I do carry a bigger a roster. I just have to carry the right players for a bigger roster - the type of players that's unselfish, that's motivated, but unselfish and understands the team's concept because they may not see playing time right away. Then it may take a little bit of time. And we do like to carry quite a few defense specialist/libero type players.

Do you normally recruit five to six every year?

That's exactly right. Five to six. People ask what position we're recruiting and for the most part we're recruiting every position every year based on... We're not on scholarship, so we don't have the 12 scholarship type players. That gives us the ability to have a few more because they're basically all paying for school, or get financial aid based on the financial need of the family.

If you were to ballpark it, of the five or six players that you get coming in, in any given year, how many of them will stick all the way through four years?

Great question. I would say four to five. If they're juniors or seniors and they aren't one of the top eight players on our team, often times they'll decide it's time better spent putting in more time at the hospital to volunteer to go to med school or something like that. I would say, out of six, four to five. We may lose one, we may lose two based on that.

Can you ballpark the level of play among the top Division III schools vis-a-vis Division I?

Sure. I like to say I think that the top 10 to 15 Division III schools play at a mid major level. I'd hate to pick specific schools but I know that when we're recruiting our athletes, they're looking at mid majors, maybe MAC conference, Ivy conference, that type of school. I don't know if you've ever had a chance to watch a clip of our finals this past year. I heard time and time again what a high level of play that was. Those are the schools that we're recruiting against - again, mid majors, MAC schools, Ivy League schools. We've gone against quite a few ACC schools. I think that's the level your top 10 or 15 schools are playing at.

It's a great level of volleyball. Often times, we may be just a little bit physically smaller. Our middles may not be 6'3", 6'4", they may be 6ft, 6'1". Our outside hitters may not touch 10 feet, they maybe touch 9'8", 9'9". Physically they might be that small. I can tell you my setter, she 6'2" and I would say she would set for the top 20 to top 40 Division I schools in the country.

Do you run a JV squad?

We do not. There are some Division III schools that do but we choose not to.

How do you keep players 10 through 22 happy?

That's a great question. One of my assistants, who coaches for the A5 18-1 team (they've had great success here), he's always said it's the happiest group of 20 players I've ever seen on a team. Everything we do is about team, whether that's practice or playing. They know how much we value them, whether it's the best on our team, or if it's #20.

We have a great staff. We have five coaches on our team. The four assistants are high level coaches. One of ours played professionally in China. Scott Shelly is an outstanding coach. I think we have a really good coaching staff. Our practices are really intense. Everybody on our team is being trained hard. I think they feel that they're personally improving and then they have to compete. I think we recruit competitors that really love the competition factor of our team. Every time they come into the practice they're going to be competing to play. If they're playing the best, they're going to play.

I also think there's so much more to our program. We have a lot of fun together. We talk about the journey more than the destination when we were travelling and doing things like that. They know how much we care and love them. Whether, like I said, they're the best player or they're #20.

Is there a link between the types of student athletes that you attract in terms of they're high achievers - obviously academically and elsewhere - and that work mindset, that drive to train and improve?

Absolutely. I was doing a recruiting seminar at the AAU Championships in Orlando and someone asked me a similar question. I do. I think there's a direct link. The high achiever academically we have found extremely competitive. They're extremely competitive on the volleyball court and off the volleyball court. I am not ever scheduling a study hall. I think they would laugh at me if I ever said something like that. Because they know when to study and how much to study. Often times I'm telling them, "Take a break. You don't need to study that long."

I do think it's a direct relationship between the two. That would be the biggest challenge, I think, that I have. When you talk about playing time, it's not that they necessarily think they should be out there, that they're the best players. They just want to be because they're high achievers.

I've got to find ways to challenge them every single day. I tell people all the time, Emory type athletes makes me a better coach because I know I need to be prepared. I know I have to set up practices that are challenging. We have to be on top of our game or they will know it. Because they're really, really intelligent and really smart. They want to be challenged, and if we don't then they don't feel good about themselves.

Obviously a big part of the mindset of Division III is that you're students first and athletes second. From that perspective, what sort of

pressures and expectations come down to you from the athletic department and the administration generally?

It's a competitive school obviously. All the sports programs here at Emory do exceptionally well. Our swimming team just won their seventh straight national championship. Our women's tennis team won a national championship last year. I think it's more pressure that we all put on ourselves.

Most of the time what we hear from administration is, "We want to provide an incredibly positive experience for our student athletes." They don't talk about the winning aspect. They really, really stress a positive experience for the student athletes here. I think the coaches that are here at Emory, we're the ones that are driven towards the winning aspect of it. I know if I lose a match I don't sleep for the next three days trying to figure out why we lost that match. It's an inner-drive, and I think all the coaches here have that same inner drive which motivates one another to continue to be successful.

It's not from the administration, and I'm thankful for that because I put enough pressure from myself. It was a little different at my previous school because you were expected to win. But thankfully we are winning here and we're winning at a really high level. If not, I think I'd be bouncing my head against the wall.

On that subject, for you is it a drive to win or is it a drive not to loose?

Wow.

Or can you not separate the two?

I've asked myself that question a lot. Sadly I think it's a drive not to lose for me, and I wish it was the other way. Yet on the other hand we lost the national championship game last year in set five. It's still to me one of the greatest seasons we've ever had for so many different reasons. I do have the internal fear of, "I don't want to lose." Because we've won at some ridiculous rate here.

That's a really good personal question, I ask myself all the time. I can tell you this, when I lose it hurts more than the excitement of winning. That's why I probably answered that question. We've had some great wins and exciting wins, but yet when I lose I seem to take it home with me a little harder.

When I was talking with Mick Haley, he talked about how his win rate when he was coaching is something like 80%. When he took over the US program ahead of the 2000 Olympics, that was his first experience of not winning 80% of his matches. They were more like 50% of the time and he said he just didn't know how to handle it. Just blew his mind for a while.

I know this past season we lost the match in the first weekend of the year, which is pretty unheard of. It's not that I'm trying to avoid people, but usually your first weekend isn't one filled with nationally ranked teams. We lost the match there. Like Mick, I had a really hard time handling it. I think we won the next 24 matches in a row, or something like that, but as soon as we lost, I made a major change in our line up. I don't think most people would panic after one loss but yet, it drove me to where I made a pretty drastic change. We went on and had an incredible season. I agree with Mick, I'm not really good or know how to handle it very well.

The question is - in hindsight obviously - was that decision critical in going 24 in a row after that? Or do you think it might not have mattered one way or the other?

Yeah, I think it was critical. We ended up having to make our All-Region outside hitter into our libero, and she had never played libero before. But it was exactly what we needed, and she was open to doing it. Then we had a third outside hitter on the bench that was still very good. I think it changed everything. Her willingness to change positions was huge for us too. If she would have balked at it or been upset about it, I don't think we would have made it to another national championship game. She ended up becoming an All-American and the crazy story is she came in as a middle blocker and she never even played back row before she got here.

Those are the fun stories.

Yeah, it's true. Just circling back a little bit to the other coaches in the department, how much collaboration and interaction do you have with them?

I think everybody has their little pockets. Our men's basketball coach, our men's tennis coach and our men's baseball coach, our offices are real close, so it's a constant collaboration of ideas, thoughts. A day doesn't go by that we're not sitting in one another's office. I was just with the men's basketball coach watching the end of the British Open and talking about being mentally tough. I can say, those three specifically for me continue to make me better, to motivate me and I think that's huge. When I was at the University of Georgia I had some great mentors around me there too that coached other sports. You have to have that to make you better. To bounce ideas off - different things like that. For me, with those three coaches it's very important.

You mentioned before part of the requirement of keeping so many players happy is that they know their role within the team and they know that they're valuable. How do you go about establishing that - making them understand it, or making them appreciate the value that you see in them and that others see - the rest of the team and the rest of the program - to encourage that sort of feeling?

Yeah, I think that's one of the most important things, and it's a really good question. I spend a lot of time with players individually. We do a lot of 1-on-1 meetings. I try to spend time with all of them before or after practice, getting to know them on a very personal basis. Once you get to know them on a very personal basis, you can make it known what's important if somebody just did an outstanding thing on campus, whether they become vice president of the student government or different things like that. I think you have to make sure you applaud that. You applaud things outside of the volleyball arena so to speak. I think it's really important to hear people, to listen to them, to value their ideas. I tell them all the time, we're a democracy. I just have to make the final decision. That's important. I just spent a lot of time talking on the phone to my rising seniors about what's important to them in their communication with the other players on the team.

I think it's listening. I think it's getting to know them. I think it's valuing who they are and then finding a really important role for them. Not just the role that's convenient, but a role that's really important to the organizational structure. We talked about it when we had four captains last year and each one of those captains had a different role - whether it's a speaking role, whether it was the organizational role, whether it was being the leader in the weight room. One of our players - out of the four seniors - one of them didn't play very much. She was responsible to keeping the team motivated in the weight room. She knew how important that was and she just grabbed it and took it, and it's probably the healthiest most in-shape we've ever been. She knows that was partly based on what she did with the team.

I think finding important roles, hearing, communicating and really getting to know them on a deeper level is the key.

You brought up the subject of captains. Do you have a process for selecting the captains? Is there any specific criteria you look for or is that something that's a bit more dynamic within any given group?

I think it's different with any given group. This year we've had two rising seniors that are both outstanding leaders. Some years we vote and we tell them when they vote we will take that into consideration, but ultimately the staff will decide, because I think it's very, very important to hear what they have to say. On the other hand, I think as a staff we know what we're looking for and what that particular team needs. We've had two captains up to four captains just based on the make up of the team. For instance,

I just asked our two rising seniors, "Do you need a third to help you lead this team?" They're talking about it amongst themselves. They're going to let me know. If they feel like they need another one, then we'll go about figuring who that's going to be. I think every team is a little bit different and we adapt our selection based on the team, not just one particular way we do it.

You mentioned the vote. Do the players know the results of the voting, or is it just for you?

It's just for us. We don't even tell them the day we're going to vote. They have to come - I know it's sounds funny - but they have to come to our assistant, tell them who they want, and then the assistant puts it up on the chalk board before anybody else see it. They can't write it on a piece of paper without their name of it. They have to own it. Then after that, we as a staff will discuss it and then we'll make the decision.

What responsibilities do you assign to your captains? You touched on this a little bit. Can you go a little further?

We give them a lot of responsibility from, again, the organization of it to integrating the new players to the team. We'll start off the season going on a team retreat. I've asked them to decide what they would like to do at that time. We're bringing in a bunch of new players. We have a large freshman class coming in. We asked them to really think about that - what's going to be important while we're away for a couple of days. We asked them to let us know as a staff if they think anything is going in the wrong direction. We have weekly captain meetings just to talk about the team and where we are, and if there's anything that we need to know. Then they oversee it at that point. You have the typical, "These are the uniforms that we're wearing on this day. These are the practice uniforms we have this day." There's that basic organization part of it. It's important for them to be that liaison between us, the bridge. They only bring things to us that they can't handle themselves or they believe we need to know.

You talk about what sounds like a lot of collaboration between the players and the staff. Do you collectively set goals, either for the group or the program and or individual players?

We collectively do that for the team. We spend time talking about our goals and that type of thing, and then or we talk specifically individually on our 1-on-1 meetings about their individual goals and their individual roles based on how that can help the team. We don't have any type of award system. We're not big on even announcing awards. Everything is based on the team. We say if the team is going to be successful, the individual awards will come.

I think it's important for, say, you want your outside hitters to hit above .300 or something like that. We have goals that we believe are attainable. We'll talk with them specifically about that - what's their passing rate and things like that. We don't have, "I want to be an All-American." Type goals.

It sounds like you try to make things objective and measurable.

Very. We don't have a thousand different goals for each person, though. I think one or two per player - whether it's defensively or block or something like that. We try to make attainable goals.

You talked a lot in terms of stats. Do you do a lot of stat work in terms of looking at comparative analytics to see what levels you need to be at, or where the team needs to be at to be competing for a national championship?

I don't do a lot of comparison with other teams. We have our specific goals that we have for our outside hitters. We want them to hit above .300. Our middle hitters, we want them to hit about .350. We want our passers passing at a certain rate. We have some different things like that.

I'm not a stat person. We talk about it as a staff all the time. We're definitely more of a feel type staff - feeling in what direction we're going. That's why I probably drive Gold Medal Squared people crazy because I'm not super,

"Put this quadrant together statistically." Of course you want them to have goals - statistical goals. If we feel like the teams is playing well and going in the right direction, then we don't pull off a stat sheet. I know that our players get online and see what their stats look like and how many kills and how many errors and different things like that. We don't make it a major focus of our team or our program.

Let's work our way through your season. You start in the latter part of August and, as you said, you begin with 2-a-days. Then once school starts it's down to one a day. What's your primary focus during that initial week or so when you're running 2-a-days?

We do try to get as many reps in as we can. Hopefully they've come pre-pared. Our players do a really good job of coming really fit and in shape. They've always done a fabulous job with that. We want to get as many reps in. The crazy thing with Division III is abbreviated pre-season. We have our first match on September 1st. We've got to get rolling pretty fast. We'll usually in the 2-a-days in the morning do a lot of rep work - a lot of passing, a lot of defense, attacking. In the afternoon, we are already getting in to 6-on-6 play. We have to do that to get ready. We feel like we've really done a good job in previous years being prepared for those first couple weeks.

It almost sounds crazy, but we get prepared and then after those couple of weeks, we come back and try to do more repetition work - as much as we can since you only have a two hour block of practice during the weekdays. We do that because our season is pretty short. We do a lot of 6-on-6 training. But anybody that wants to come in for extra reps, we're always there to do that because we don't have that long of a practice time.

I also like to taper my team. I think we've done a great job of this in the past. We're playing our best in November. In September, early October, we're practicing two and a half hours. As we get to mid-October, end of October, two hours. And when we get into conference championship and NCAA finals and regionals we're never going more than an hour and a half at our practices.

Do you script pre-season, or do you plan it day-by-day?

I definitely plan it day-by-day. We'll look at it as a staff and we'll get to-gether as a staff and we'll say, "Okay, here's our 16 practice opportunities. We need to get this done by this day. We'll give ourselves to Day 4 to implement this." Then we'll say, "By Day 8, we've got to implement this. By Day 12 ... " That kind of thing.

We'll give ourselves our goals as a team, but we won't go and say, "This is specifically what we're doing at practice this day." I'm a big believer - I even heard Russ Rose say this - we don't do a lot of things. We do a small amount of things a lot of times. I have my favorite type drills and my favourite type of team training and we'll stick to that most of the time. I don't just create new drills to do new drills. Again, we'll do a small amount of things a lot of times.

To that point, do you feel any pressure from the squad to mix the drills up? To do something different from time to time?

I do. Because you know because you've worked with these type of student athletes. They want to pushed. They want to be motivated. I do think they want a variety and often times, whether that's a new kind of scoring game that you'll create a different scoring system, or something like that. You're still doing a similar drill, but you create a different scoring system which will present a different challenge for them. Yes, I do feel that. I never wanted to walk into practice and do the same thing every single time. On the other hand, you know to do something similar, you're going to get better and better at it.

I feel that a little bit because of the type of student-athletes that I work with. On the other hand, we also know what's best for them with muscle memory and specific training. You've got to get good at specific things. I'm big on eliminating errors and reducing errors. We'll do a lot of out-of-sys-tem training type things. I think if you eliminate errors and play defense, you've got a pretty good chance to win those sets. We'll do a lot of that because I believe in it. Things like that.

What does your typical week look like schedule-wise between training and matches?

We usually are playing Friday's and Saturdays. We will start practice on Monday. Practice Monday, Tuesday, Wednesday, Thursday or travel Thursday. We'll be practicing 3:00 to 6:00. If we're travelling on Thursday then we'll usually get to the site and do a short serving & pass for an hour, or something like that. Play Friday and Saturday.

Division III is a little bit different in that we will play three to four matches in a weekend. Then we'll always have off on Sunday. If we play Saturday-Sunday then we'll always have off on Monday. We'll lift twice a week. Our strength coach does an amazing job. We'll do a maintenance type program throughout the Fall - lifting only about 30 minutes twice a week. We'll do something like that. That's pretty much the general schedule that we have.

What's the intensity level of your trainings between Monday and Thursday, assuming you're not travelling Thursday?

I would say Monday through Wednesday we train very hard. Maybe towards the end of the season it'll be a little bit lighter on Monday based on travel or based on play. Really hard Tuesday and Wednesday. A little bit lighter - a lot of the times staying on the ground - Thursday if we're playing on Friday. Or more of serving and passing, staying on the ground, not jumping or jumping minimally on Thursday. A little bit shorter practice but we definitely go hard Monday, Tuesday, and Wednesday.

I believe in conditioning by playing volleyball. We're not going to be out there sprinting. And yes, we're going to be lifting because of injury prevention, but I believe our conditioning is done within the framework of volleyball.

Do you look at any peaks during the course of your season, or do you look at it more as a single progression?

I look at it more a single progression. I'm always looking towards November. I do in the middle of the season, give them a three day break. If I really feel like the need it, we've given them a four day break. A little bit unheard of. They'll have Friday, Saturday, Sunday off. I always take off a weekend. Based on where the team is, if it's our Fall Break I might give them a little bit more time. Right after that break, I always know that we're going to struggle a little bit for the next week or so. After that we really start climbing back up and really get our legs and really start peaking. We're always talking about November. Even we prepare for that school-wise. We prepare of that fitness-wise. We prepare for that travelling wise.

Our team, you always hear them talking about November. "We got to get ready for November." That's been really successful for us to focus that way, going in that direction. I do know mid-season, I try to take a three to four day break.

All right, just to make sure we've got our framework for this. Can you describe what the NCAA tournament qualification process is in Division III?

There are 62 to 63 teams, based on how many teams are in Division III at the time. I think we're near 450. I think last year we were at 63 in the tournament. Every year it's based on the percentage of it. There's a majority ... I think it was close to 47, 48 automatic qualifiers. Then we have anywhere from 13 to 16 at-large bids. For instance, our conference last year ... We won our conference. We got the AQ, but Washington University in St. Louis and The University of Chicago both got at-large bids. Then they're usually two to three bids for ... It's called pool C. They aren't part of a conference. There's a couple of bids for those schools that aren't in a conference. That makes up the field of 63. Like I said it could be 64 based on the number, because Division III is increasing every year.

[Editors Note: Division III works on a regional structure where teams are placed into regional brackets based on their location. Division II works in a similar way. Division I differs in that there is an initial seeding process to place teams in the brackets.]

Completely unrelated but sidetrack question. How are you in the same conference with a school in St. Louis?

Well, our league actually is the most spread out conference in the country besides the conference that includes Hawaii. Twenty-five years, or maybe 26 years ago, the presidents of major research institutions decided that they wanted to put together a conference of the top research institutions in the country. That included University of Chicago, Washington University in St. Louis, University of Rochester, New York University, Carnegie Mellon, Case Western. At that time Johns Hopkins was in that as well. The presidents got together and it's as phenomenal conference. All those prioritize academics, and they're large research institutions. It's a major commitment from the universities travel-wise, budgetary-wise to be in this conference. It is without question really one of the best conferences I think in the country in Division III.

Sounds like a Division III version of the Ivy League with a much bigger footprint.

Very similar, exactly.

Going back to the season stuff, what does a typical training session look like in September versus what it might look like in November?

In September I would say, we get to practice, again maybe two and a half hours. We would start off 25-30 minutes with intense ball control. Whether that's something pepper-like - 3-person pepper, long court pepper - anything ball control related. Whether that's partners or 3-person or a type thing that you have three in the back, a setter in the front. A lot of intense ball control type things. Then we probably spend 25-35 minutes serving and passing. Lots of time and intense focus on that, but usually a competitive type serving and passing with a lot of repetitions. Then we would go to some sort of 6-on-6 - whether that's a serve receive type game like baseball or a wash type game. We would usually end on some normal volleyball. Either that's a fifth set or a 22-22 win by two set. Something like that.

As we get a little bit further into the season, our ball control would go 10-15 minutes, our serve receive would still be 15-20 minutes. We would so some sort of scheme based on who we're playing, some sort of scouting. "We're going to be doing this against this opponent." Then we would finish off 30-45 minutes in the 6-on-6 training atmosphere.

What do your warmups look like?

Different every time. I usually have 3-4 different warmups. We'll start with a dynamic stretch and our Strength & Conditioning coach puts that together - 5 to 10 minutes of dynamic stretch. It's pretty standard. We think stretching after is more important than stretching before. Then we get into the ball-handling.

You're ball-handling is basically an extension of your warmup?

Absolutely. We'll do a lot of cooperative ball-handling things. Something usually cooperative like left side peppers, so they're transitioning, something like that.

Just to put this in context. What does your training facility look like?

We have a really great training facility. Our main gym has five courts, we usually never use five courts max. We would use three. We also have three outstanding courts upstairs, so we have a total of eight. We use two to three courts for practice, and actually towards the end of the season, we're usually just on one court because we don't need more than that at the time. It's our weight room, our locker room, our training facility and even our pool all in the same site. We're very fortunate with what we have here.

You talked about doing opponent scouting. Do you train A-team versus B-team?

Most of the time we do. We also do a lot of A-front row versus A-front row. We're trying hard to compete against the best, so we'll our front middle versus our front middle [meaning first team MBs against each other] with the defenses behind us. We do a lot of training that way. I believe it's really important to do that. Like you said, if you see anybody getting down or you've got to find that right person ... Our second team setter this year was a really highly motivated kid and she kept them going hard. I think that's probably what's made us better. You've got to get the right mix on the other side that's still going to go hard versus your starting team.

When you're going 6-on-6, what are the other eight players doing?

I wave a lot through. If we're going against our second team, I'm using two middles in the front and they're rotating, and two defenders and left back and they're rotating. If the level doesn't fall off, I'm trying to incorporate them. I'm trying to put left side hitters when a wash point scores they switch. I'm putting the second team into the best situation I can to compete against our first team.

Now, if we have players that aren't at the same level and it's going to take the level of the scrimmage down, I'm not going to use them.

Obviously you've spoken with them.

Yeah, absolutely. They know coming in that we're going to play the best players - whether that's best 12 that's going to practice or the best 14. They know that ahead of time.

In terms of playing time what's your philosophy on sharing that around through the course of the season?

I'm not big on that. We don't play people just to play them, and don't get experience if we think that's not going to help us in the end. I'm not a coach that's going to put somebody in for the last three points or something like that. I feel like you have to earn it. If they've earned it, and it's going to prepare us for if we need a third hitter, we need a big energy person to come in, we're going to do that.

Again, I just don't play people to play them. I think we're going to play them if we feel like it's going to make us better. Maybe that means the whole second team is going to play against a weaker team if we feel like we need to get them experienced then we'll do it. You have to earn the right to play in our program.

You said you've got 15 training opportunities in the Spring, what's your main focus there?

Especially the newer kids, that's the time that we're doing our best. Whether it's the changed technique, change in arm swing, that's the time that we're really spending with our younger players because we didn't have time to do that in the Fall. It may be changing a technique to getting some of our younger players reps. And our spring tournament, that's when we do try to play everybody and give them that opportunity to play.

You said your kids come in fit for pre-season, so it sounds like you get pretty good buy-in in terms of off-season training. Do you ever have any issues with that? I know in my experience there were some players who were a little hesitant about the weight lifting side of things. "I don't want to get big." That's sort of thing. Do you ever run into any issues with individual players?

I did about 10 years ago, but I think culture has changed so much that I haven't had that problem in a really, really long time. We do have a great buy-in and I think our strength coach does an amazing job of educating them that, "You're not going to get big, you're actually going to get leaner if you do this right." Young women with the pressures out there ... It's hard because of what they read and what they see. But again, I think our strength staff does an amazing job of just educating them that, "Okay this isn't going to get you bigger, this actually is going to help you." Those types of things. We haven't had that in probably 10 years.

I guess this winds things to a more specific focus. How technical are you with your training? You obviously do a lot of 6s, but how precise do you want your players to be with their mechanics?

Probably from 1 to 10 - 10 being the most - I'm probably at 2. I believe there's lots of different ways to do things. I think there's keys to each skill. For instance, obviously I think with passing, getting your platform out ready and directing your platform to target. I think there's those have-tos in certain skills.

Yes, we have our outside hitter that has the craziest arm swing, but nobody can block her because it's the craziest arm swing. She does it extremely, well so I'm surely not going to change her.

I'm not super technical. Again I would probably be really low on the scale of technical coaches, because I think there's a lot of different ways to get to the end point. There are some of those absolutes. In approach you've got to go slow to fast and be dynamic. I'm not going to allow someone to go at the same speed on their approach, but yet I'm going to let people have different arm swings. Everybody's body is a little bit different and does things differently.

Blocking, I'm not a swing blocker, but we've had a player, a middle, that has some swing blocking technique to her that's the way she was trained. As long as we can do it within our system what she has perfected, I'm okay with that.

You mentioned the approach thing, but are there certain triggers where you say, "Okay I need to intervene here."

Yeah, there's definitely different things like that. We have ... Trying to think of one.

One of our incoming freshmen is a topspin server, but she's not able to get the velocity on the topspin to make it beneficial for herself. She's not going to be a topspin server for us anymore. We're not going to give the other team free balls. I know it sounds simple, but she's going to go to jump float. That's going to be more productive for us than topspin at 26 miles per hour.

Do you have any issues or many issues with overuse injuries?

Yeah, some of these players that come in from these clubs that just train so long and so hard, we do. Some shoulders, some knees. So that's an issue with long, long practices. That's another reason I think some of these high level players are choosing Division III, because there's balance in Division III. Our seasons are a little bit shorter, our spring season is very short. It allows them to continue to play, but yet their bodies are able to recover.

Going back to your training, how much relative time do you allocate to sideout work versus transition, and in-system versus out-of-system?

That's a great question. I would say that's pretty equal. One day we'll be working on siding-out. The next day we'll be working on defending. We work a lot on transition. I probably lean to that direction, but I think you have to spend equal time on both.

Do you have any consistent keys to success at your level?

I do.

For me, what I found to be the key is for our style of play we have to get very fast dynamic players. We've brought some bigger, so to speak, slower players into our program - maybe the 6'3", 6'4" kid - and I found that they weren't very successful here. What we do, we play a very high tempo, very fast type offense. Our speed is what makes our team go. If I try to fit a bigger player into that system, it hasn't worked. [We bring] fast, quick, and then really hardworking players into our system. We play very high energy, super excited. If you saw our team - the way they play - they're very high energy, they're very fast, and I think that that's what signifies our program.

A little bit more specific now, are there key facets for the game, where you say, "Okay this sort of thing is what is going to make the difference between us contending for the national championship this year and maybe finishing second in our league."?

I think a lot of it wraps around our setter. We've had eight straight years of All-Americans setters. We put a lot on our setter, and pretty much educate her and let her go and let her lead the team. We've had great, great, great leaders in that position. I know for our recruiting class we are looking to bring in our next leader. If somebody was to look at our program the last few years they would think things really are wrapped around that position for us.

The other thing we've always had great middle hitters in our program. Not that I don't believe the key is outside hitters, but our middles and our setters have seemed to be really a great foundation for us.

You brought up the setter education idea. What sorts of things do you work on specifically in that regard?

Like specifically, she and I will sit down and work through all our rotations - 1 through 6. We'll sit down and we'll talk about them at length, about what she's feeling out of this rotation, what place she has most confidence in. Why? We'll talk about blocking match ups that we may see. We'll sit down and really talk through the game with her and then we let her go.

I know when I was at Georgia, Jim called a lot of the plays in serve receive and a lot of coaches still do that. We don't do that. We try to educate her and then let her play. We want her focus on the game, her opponents, but we've got to prepare her for that. We spend a lot of time just talking about our philosophy, what we want to get out of the set, who we have most confidence in, when the game is on the line. It seems to work. Like I said if she gets All-American again it will be eight straight years of all American setters. For us it's been the key to success.

When do you start that process with the setter? Assuming that a setter isn't a starter as a freshman, are you still already getting her into that thought process?

No. Most of time we're just working with our starting setter, to be honest with you. Whoever the next setter is - like our setter this year, this will be her last season - we would spend the majority of the time in the Spring with our setter that we expect to take over.

This might be somewhat related, do you do video assessments with the team in terms of looking at the opposition?

We scout as a staff. Then we put our game plan together and then we share that one with them, for a couple reasons. First of all, we don't want them worrying about the other side of the net too much. We want them just worried about our side and what we can do. We feel like if we play well then we'll beat the majority of the teams.

We as a staff prepare ourselves. So we know who we want to serve. So we know who we want to go after at the net. We know all those different things, and we'll communicate that tune throughout the match. We don't want to put too much in their heads. We want them to just be thinking about their game and our team, and then we'll take care of the other side.

Do you use video in training itself?

We use video at practice. Literally taking video of them and showing them right there. Because they have so much school work, we don't bring anybody in for extra video sessions or anything like that, but we'll be at practice with our iPad. We'll take a clip of them passing or something like that. We'll immediately have them walk over and take a look at it. That's how we use most of our videoing.

Let's talk a bit about recruiting. You've touched on it a little bit, but how does your calendar work in terms of your recruiting efforts. I'm guessing its 12 months like everybody else.

It's absolutely 12 months. We start in August, during the season. You're having kids coming visit during the Fall to watch you play. As soon as the Fall is done, you know you're jumping into the recruiting pretty much starting in January. We try to take December off, even though there's a few things going on.

In January you usually have the early club tournaments, whether in Phoenix or wherever they may be. Then we are going to hit all the major qualifiers, whether it's Las Vegas, L.A., all the major qualifiers or JVA type events. We usually go to 10-12 of the major events, plus thankfully a lot is here in Atlanta. There's a lot of things that come through Atlanta.

Then during the Spring we are hosting tons and tons of visits. Kids just come in and visit again. Whether it's their first or second visit we're hosting. I think we hosted close to 70 kids last Spring.

During the summer you're going to JOs and you're going to AAUs and you're finished that up the first week of July. Then we host our camps here. We just got to finish with a lead camp. We had 75 players fly in from all over the country. That's a great opportunity for them to see our campus, meet our coaches, meet our players. We've had great success with our Lead camp.

Then take about a week or two off and you start again with your season in August.

In terms of your staff, do you have somebody else as a recruiting co-ordinator, or with primary responsibility for recruiting? Or is it something that you'd share around?

We share it. We do have a full-time assistant, which I'm very fortunate with. Not all Division III schools have that. We share in the recruiting process.

He does a lot of data entry and we both pretty much have our hands fully in with the recruiting process. When I was at Georgia I was the full-time recruiting coordinator. That was purely my main responsibility, but I like to be involved in that part of it because it's really important to me. That may be why that we equally are part of it.

In terms of staff selection, do you have an approach that you use in terms of identifying who you want to bring in - the type of people that you want to bring into the staff? I bring it up from the perspective of some people look at themselves and say, "Okay I am this type of person. I should have this other type of person in the staff with me." Whereas other people just want to look for who are the best candidates I can bring in and then we'll go from there.

That's such a great point. I know who I am and I'm pretty demanding and very much Type-A. I definitely have to find someone - let's put it this way - able to deal with me, so that's super important. We've really had a positive staff. We are not yellers. We believe we're more of teachers, mentors, role models. We have to have people in our staff that believe that same thing.

Oftentimes I've got to get assistant coaches that are more technical than I am. As I mentioned earlier in the conversation, I'm not very technically focused, so I do bring in assistants that I know are much more technically savvy than myself. That's super important. But we're really organized, we are super disciplined about things within our programs.

How do you divide out the responsibilities between the staff?

I just base on strengths. For our one assistant Helen Lynn, she played professionally in China. She was on the junior national team. She's outstanding teaching defense and passing. We give her that main responsibility. My full-time assistant Joe Gibson, his strength is blocking. So we give him that and our other coach Scott Shelly - who's very offensive minded - he oversees the setting and the offense. It's really based on the strengths, and if there is something not covered specifically, I'll take that part of the game. But I over see the team as a whole within building the framework as 6-person units.

I'm assuming that over the years you've been approached, or at least had the idea discussed with you, that you move on from Emory to Division I or Division II or whatever. What's that's been like for you in the decision-making along the way?

I guess it was probably tougher maybe 10 years ago. I was blessed with some really neat opportunities to go back to my alma mater at the University of Georgia a few times. I had some really, really neat other opportunities out there, but every time I seriously looked at it my heart just kept me here. I love working with this type of student. I love competing for a national championship every year. I like our athletes that come here really believe in balance. My family is super important to me. I have a lot of nieces and nephews that I travel around the country watching playing sports in college. I wanted that same balance. Every time I got close - I was really close to going back to University of Georgia couple of times - I just kept getting pulled back here, and I'm really thankful that I did.

Well, you can't argue with it. If you're happy then stick with it.

There's a lot of people out there that are in the Big 10 and SEC and ACC that keep telling me every time I see them that I've got the best job in the world, so in some ways I truly believe that.

This ties in with the idea that we need more women in coaching, we need more women at the top level of coaching. Do you ever feel any pressure from the female coaching community, or more broadly to be at a top Division I program?

I do and I did both of them. I really felt like that. I think at this point for the most part people know that I'm probably not going anywhere. Then, on the other hand, maybe 8-9 years ago I really felt that pressure like I need to go out there and do that. We need to get more women at that level and different things like that.

I'm staying now, so I don't feel it is much, but there was a time I did feel that way - that I have to get out there and help women and get more opportunities for women out there. But it is tough, because especially women running families and doing all that stuff, the demands are just increasing and increasing. It's getting more and more difficult to do it at that level and to be able to raise kids. Unless you have an incredibly supportive husband.

I know Lizzy Stemke at Georgia [now former head coach], a very good friend of mine. Her husband is amazing and is obviously very active in raising their children ,so she can do what she's doing. It takes some incredible family to be able to do it at that level.

Let's wind back the machine a little bit further. Can you look back and see a change or a path of development in the way you've coached over the years?

I think I'm a lot more patient now then I was when I was young. I think that's one thing - I'm a lot more patient. I see the big picture more than I did before. I was so focused on winning national championships and getting back to the finals and different things like that. Obviously, I still want to do that, and I love being able to do that. But I also think I see the big picture that it's not all about winning, although I'm very motivated to do that. Are they having great experience, are we becoming the best that we can possibly be? I think I've become more patient. I'm seeing the big picture. Why we are doing this? I'd say that mostly.

What about in the way you do your training? Have you changed that meaningfully over the years?

Yeah, I think I've leaned more towards the 6-on-6 training. I think earlier on in my career I thought I was just supposed to sort of rep it out. Just rep, rep, rep, rep, rep. I felt like I was supposed to be doing that as opposed to what I believe I was most passionate about and training 6-on-6. I think you can train those things within the context of 6-on-6 play. I just started saying, "I don't really care what anybody else is doing, this is what I believe in." I think we do a lot more competing in 6-on-6 than I did earlier on in my career.

You've mentioned talking with your peers in the athletic department and having your mentors in volleyball more broadly. What other things do you do to maintain your own development as a coach?

I do obviously the conventions. I have a lot of great friends in the college volleyball world that I'm constantly talking to on the phone and bouncing ideas off of them. I'm on the internet a lot watching coaches. YouTube is fantastic for watching people doing drills or doing sessions. I think the AVCA does a great job of educating with web casts and different things.

Reading books - I'm just reading Thinking Volleyball by Mike Hebert which is a great book. It's totally not a skills book. It's thinking volleyball, thinking outside the box. I love reading. I love following different coaches, different things John Wooden has written. I love coach K from Duke, different things like that. I'm constantly trying to learn, not just about the game of volleyball, but about coaching and motivating.

What advice do you have or would you give to somebody who is in the developmental stage of their career, say the first three to five years?

One of the best things that I think I ever did in the first 3-5 years was going around working as many camps as I was able to do, and getting to know people. I think still the best thing I've ever done was go work the Kentucky camps when I was a GA. When Kathy DeBoer, Mary Wise and Sharon Dingman, that was the staff there. I got to know them, who catapulted and helped my career. Obviously, continue to network through the AVCA convention just getting to know people.

The other thing I think young coaches should do, especially in the Spring is travel around. Go spend 2-3 days learning from someone's program. If you ask John Dunning, "Can I come there for two or three days and watch your practices at Stanford?" I guarantee he would be more than willing to let you do that. I would go and I'd watch people run practices and talk to them as much as I could. Go to the AVCA conventions and just watch and learn. I do think the Summer is a great opportunity to go connect with people through camps as well.

I think a lot of people might be surprised at how ready even top coaches are to have people come and visit and just hang out in the gym and watch what's going on.

Yeah it's amazing, I know Karch said that when they're training come watch them [the USA Women] train in L.A. I'm telling you if I lived in that area, I would be down there once a week watching that.

Yeah, me too probably.

It's surprising to me that people don't do that more often.

That brings up something that's come up in other interviews. It's that some coaches get this idea where it's their team or it's their club or their program or whatever and they're just focused on that and they ignore all the external stuff. They just want to be their own little fief or whatever. Is that something that you see?

Yes and no. First of all it's not the way we think here. We're always trying to do coaching clinics. We are always trying to grow the game. We are always trying ... We tell all high school coaches and any of the college coaches around here, "If you ever want to come into our gym, come to our gym. Ask us questions, do all these things."

I've heard that at a higher level people are unwilling to share their ideas and different things like that. That's just not the way we are. Anybody I've ever asked questions have always been open and willing to talk. I haven't seen that, I've heard, but I haven't seen that personally.

I remember I was recruiting one time - I think it was in Indianapolis - and I just went up to the bar in an Olive Garden or something like that to have dinner and Christy Johnson from Iowa State was like two seats over and we started talking and having a great conversation. She didn't know who I was and she was so willing to share ideas and things like that. I'd never felt that way but I hear that from other folks.

Please post a review

Did you find these interviews interesting, educational, inspiring, and/or insightful?

If so, please leave a review wherever you go to get your books. Reviews help prospective future readers in their decision-making process. Books with more reviews tend to get more attention as well. We want to positively influence the coaching careers of as many women as we can with Wizard Women, so the more people we can reach, the greater the impact we can have.

Of course we'd love it if you post a review on social media or whatever platform you have (blog, podcast, etc.). If you let us know about it, we'll share it. Just either tag us or send the link to author@volleyballcoaching wizards.com.

Thanks! We really appreciate it.

More Wizard Women

This collection of interviews barely scratches the surface of all the out-standing women who are currently coaching in our sport and who have done so before. As noted in the Introduction, two legends – Teri Clemens and Ruth Nelson – were featured in our initial book. More are among those we interviewed in our initial cycle of Wizards work. We encourage you to check them out for even more insights and inspiration.

Visit volleyballcoachingwizards.com or you favorite book seller.

Help the Wizard Women project

While the coaches profiled here are certainly outstanding examples, they are far from the only ones who deserve recognition for their performance and achievements. Nor are they the only ones whose stories will educate and inspire current and future women in coaching. As such we want to continue developing more of these interviews. We could use some assistance to that end, though.

Identify candidates

The first way you can help is to identify potential future interviewees for us. While we can certainly identify coaches who have received high levels of recognition (e.g. national hall of fame induction), there are plenty of coaches out there doing great work in relative obscurity with great stories to tell. Those are the women we need the most assistance identifying. This is especially true for those coaching in under-represented communities. Our basic requirements are that they have at least 10 years of experience as a head coach (though we do make exceptions for long-tenured assistant coaches) and that they are currently active or have only just recently retired.

Recommendations need not be limited to just Wizard Women candidates. We're happy to get suggestions for the broader project where male and retired coaches are welcome.

Conduct interviews

We're actively looking for people who can help us further the Wizards project by conducting interviews as it allows us to develop them more quickly. For Wizard Women we are obviously looking for female interviewees, though for the broader project there is no such requirement. Having your own coaching experience is a valuable asset in this work, though that can be overcome in other ways.

If you have thoughts on a future interviewee and/or would like to be considered to be an interviewer, drop us a line at author@volleyballcoachingwizards.com. We'll be glad to hear from you.

About the Authors

Lauren Bertolacci is currently the head coach for the Swiss professional women's team Viteos NUC Volleyball, as well as being the head coach for the Swiss Women's National Team. At NUC her teams have won three straight league championships and three straight Cup titles, and have competed in CEV competition as well. Before NUC, she was the head coach for the Volley Luzern men's team. Prior to taking charge of Switzerland she assisted with the national teams of both Canada and her native Australia. Lauren's coaching career follows a professional playing career, as well as national team experience.

John Forman is the author of the well-respected Coaching Volleyball blog (CoachingVB.com) and the co-developer of Volleyball Coaching Wizards with his partner Mark Lebedew. His coaching experience includes time in all three NCAA Divisions, as well as at the 2-year college level. He also coached in England at both the university (BUCS) and National League (NVL) Division I levels, and had a stint as head coach in Sweden's top women's league. Additionally, John was a Juniors club director and coach in the New England area for several years. He's also had the good fortune of being a visiting at youth, collegiate, professional, and national teams in a number of different countries.

www.ingramcontent.com/pod-product-compliance
Lightning Source LLC
Chambersburg PA
CBHW020442130626
46549CB00001B/268